/ 14

BRUGES

CONTENTS

ART ENTHUSIASTS

Admire Flemish Primitives, Bosch and the Symbolists at the Groeninge (route 4), see Hans Memling's work in St John's Hospital (route 5), and marvel at van Eyck's altarpiece in Ghent (route 15).

RECOMMENDED ROUTES FOR...

ESCAPING THE CROWDS

Follow the lapping waters of the Langerei to the charming museum of Our Lady of the Pottery church (route 9), wander the district west of 't Zand (route 11) or cycle up the canal to peaceful Damme (route 12).

CHILDREN

Wander along canals past fishermen and houseboats on the way to the Astrid Park (route 7), visit the adorable Folklore Museum (route 6) or take to the beach at Ostend (route 13).

FOOD AND DRINK

Chocoholics will get a tasty treat at Choco-Story (route 3), while beer-lovers should sample the only beer still brewed in Bruges at the Half Moon Brewery (route 5). For seafood, nothing beats Ostend (route 13).

GREEN SPACES

Discover a real secret garden, the Hof Sebrechts Park (route 10), enjoy a picnic in the shade at tranquil Astrid Park (route 7) or explore a village surrounded by green fields and polder in Damme (route 12).

HISTORIANS

Stalk the haunts of medieval merchants (route 8), inspect the crusader's trophy that inspires religious devotion at the Holy Blood Basilica (route 3) or revisit the tragedy of World War I around Ypres (route 14).

RAINY DAYS

Situated side by side, the Groeninge, Arentshuis and Gruuthuse museums are ideal for an indoor day (route 4), or travel to Ypres, for the excellent In Flanders Fields Museum and Sanctuary Wood (route 14).

ROMANTIC BRUGES

Watch swans glide over the mirror-like Minnewater, or 'Lake of Love' (route 5), or set out early to enjoy uninterrupted views from the Rozenhoedkaai and along leafy Groenerei (route 7).

INTRODUCTION

An introduction to Bruges's geography, customs and culture, plus illuminating background information on cuisine, history and what to do when you're there.

The canals are just as atmospheric at night

EXPLORE BRUGES

Medieval Bruges is one of Europe's most romantic destinations. Canals meander around gabled almshouses, Gothic churches, world-class art galleries and boutique hotels, all packaged in a central district less than 2km (1.25 miles) across.

Bruges – Brugge to its residents – is a provincial town that hit the big time with its cloth trade in the Middle Ages, riding high for 400 years before sinking into oblivion, cut off from the world. Centuries on, 19th-century heritage enthusiasts chanced upon the time-capsule city and shook it from its Sleeping Beauty slumber, restoring it to a splendour that celebrates the Gothic and Baroque, Renaissance and modern.

The city may live off its past but it is not content to reside there. A startlingly modern music venue, incessant property renovation, chic new restaurants and a lively programme of contemporary dance, experimental music and film disprove accusations that it is little more than a museum piece. Yes, tourism dominates the city, but it is fantastically easy to escape the crowds.

GEOGRAPHY

This city of around 20,000 people is located 11km (7 miles) from the North Sea coast and is the capital of West Flanders, a province that contains the entire 67km (42 miles) of Belgium's coastline and is bordered by France, the Netherlands and the provinces of Hainaut (in French-speaking Wallonia) and East Flanders.

With the reclaimed polders of the maritime plain to the north and west, and sandy pastoral land to the east and south, the municipality of Bruges includes three distinct areas: the historic centre (a Unesco World Heritage Site), contained by a 7km- (4-mile) long ring canal along the line of the former city walls; the suburbs, named after historic parishes situated outside the walls: Sint-Michiels, Sint-Andries, Sint-Jozef and so on; and a tongue of land stretching north to the sea, including the village of Lissewege and the port of Zeebrugge.

As long as you are within the centre, and there is little reason to venture outside, the only sensible means of getting around is on foot or by bike.

HISTORY

The city grew up from a Gallo-Roman settlement, Bruggia, first mentioned in AD851. It rose to prominence as a cloth town and trading hub, its weavers renowned for their skill in transforming

The Procession of the Holy Blood occurs every year on Ascension day

English wool into the finest tapestries and garments in Europe.

Fortunes waxed and waned with time and tides. Fierce coastal storms opened and closed the city's access to the sea starting in the 11th century, when silting prevented ships from sailing directly into the centre. A flood in 1134 created a new sea route from the Zwin inlet to Damme, 7km (4 miles) to the north-east. Bruges made Damme its outer port, and dug canals to ferry goods to and from the city on small barges.

Golden Age

From 1200–1400, the city was an important member of the Hanseatic League, a network of trading cities across Europe. Foreign merchants built grand consulates and settled here, trading metals, fur and wine for locally produced cloth. The city saw the birth of the world's first stock exchange, and became a cultish place of pilgrimage, inspired by a supposed relic of Christ's blood brought back from the Crusades (and still presented for veneration in a basilica built for the purpose). The Gothic City Hall and many churches and mansions survive from this period.

Wealth and religious devotion promoted a flourishing artistic community: painters Jan van Eyck and Hans Memling made Bruges their home, catering to the court of the dukes of Burgundy, successors to the counts of Flanders and great patrons of the arts. Their rule was renowned as a period of refinement and festivities: banquets, tournaments and processions helped local craftsmen diversify into illuminated manuscripts, lace and other luxury items.

Also noteworthy, the first printed book in English was produced in Bruges in 1473 by William Caxton for Margaret, duchess of Burgundy and sister of English kings Edward IV and Richard III.

Decline

Protracted conflicts between the royal houses of England and France eventually took their toll on a city ruled by the French yet dependent on English wool. Disputes between the citizens and their rulers were compounded by the silting up of the sea-channel. By the early 16th century, Bruges was effectively cut off from the world. Courtiers and merchants abandoned the town, while religious wars and persecution forced many skilled craftsmen to flee.

Disaster then has brought riches today, as centuries of decline left many historic monuments untouched. By the mid-18th century, the much-dwindled population survived by making lace, a cottage industry that was eventually decimated by industrialisation.

Modern era

Belgian independence and the arrival of the railway brought early tourists travelling from Ostend to Brussels – many of them English people en route to the Waterloo battlefield – who came

Bruges rooftops and stepped gables

DON'T LEAVE BRUGES WITHOUT...

Seeing the work of the Flemish Primitives. Artists working in Flanders in the 15th and early 16th centuries were named 'Primitives' by 19th-century art historians, not due to any lack of sophistication, but because they developed a new technique in painting, using oils rather than tempera. Greatly admired and copied by Italian painters of the time, their style formed a bridge between the art of the medieval period and the Renaissance. The Groeninge Museum is the best place to learn more about them. See page 43.

Sightseeing from the water. It may be touristy, but taking a tour in one of the small armada of open-topped motorboats that navigate the central canal network is a great way to get a unique view of the city. The boats, many of which come with an English-speaking guide, operate daily from Mar–Nov 10am–6pm, with exceptions. Boats depart from Rozenhoedkaai, Steenhouwersdijk, Dijver, Nieuwstraat and Mariastraat. Warm clothing is advised, and you will need to duck when passing under low bridges. See page 128.

Taking a ride in a horse-drawn carriage. Similarly touristy but romantic nonetheless, a tour in one of Bruges' iconic fiacres will give you a great overview of the city and may make you feel as if you've been transported back to Bruges of yesteryear. See page 129.

Trying chips from the Frites van. Do as the locals do and opt for that Belgian favourite budget munch on the go – Belgian chips straight from the Frites van. Eat them open, standing up by the van, to be properly authentic. To find out more about Belgian fries, you can also visit the Fries Museum, in the Merchants' Quarter. See page 17 and page 61.

Testing the local brew. Belgium is rightly famed for its beer, and you can learn all about it at Bruges's only surviving brewery, De Halve Maan (Half Moon Brewery), which also has a museum. See page 47.

Paying homage to the area's fallen heroes. You can take tours to the battlefields around Ypres and, if you would like to find details of individual burial locations, you can contact the body responsible for maintaining Commonwealth war graves (www.cwgc.org). See page 129.

Visiting the city's outstanding museums. Bruges has plenty to keep culture vultures busy, with the collection at the Groeninge Museum, which follows the development of art in the Low Countries from the 15th to the 21st century, the jewel in its artistic crown. The Groeninge is just one of many museums that are part of the city museum historical sites network, and may be visited using the good-value combined City Card available from the Tourist Office. See page 43.

Learning more about Belgian chocolate. If you've got a sweet tooth and fancy learning more about one of Belgium's best exports, check out Choco-Story, which ends with a tasting session. See page 18.

Our Lady of the Pottery   *At the Groeninge Museum*

across this time-warped city. A heritage movement was launched, Gothic buildings and historic monuments were repaired, and the tourist industry took off.

CLIMATE

Bruges has the warm summers and mild winters typical of a maritime temperate climate. Snow is rare, but rain is common. July and August are the warmest months, with an average maximum of 22°,C (72°F), and temperatures hovering around 30°C (86°F) on the hottest days. June is sunniest. The coldest months are December to February, when daily averages hover at 1–5°C (34–41°F). On the chilliest days, bitter winds from the north and east can sweep across the flat polder landscape of Flanders, and make the damp air seem colder still.

While its proximity to the coast tends to keep the air fresh and clear, Bruges's canals create a locally humid environment characterised by magical mists and fog on cool evenings. Less romantically, there can be a lot of mosquitoes in summer.

POLITICS AND ECONOMICS

Bruges is the capital of West Flanders, one of 10 provinces in Belgium, a constitutional monarchy with a federal parliamentary system. The king is the head of state, while the prime minister is the head of government, leading a multi-party coalition of ministers, half of whom represent each of the Flemish and the French-speaking communities.

The main political families split in the 1970s into separate parties aligned along linguistic grounds: in Flanders, the right-wing Liberals are represented by the VLD, the socially conservative Christian Democrats by the CD&V and the Socialists by the SP.A. There is also a Green Party and a strong nationalist and far-right movement. Coalitions are very much the norm, with both the mayor of Bruges, Christian Democrat Patrick Moenaert, and the federal prime minister, Socialist Elio di Rupo, heading broad political coalitions.

Flemish autonomy

Flanders has enjoyed a degree of autonomy ever since Charlemagne divided his kingdom in AD843 and created the County of Flanders. The wealthy medieval cities won their own charters and liberties, despite often bitter dispute with the French-speaking aristocracy. After living under French, Habsburg, Spanish and Dutch rule, independence in 1830 crowned Leopold of Saxe-Coburg-Gotha as king of the Belgians, reaffirming French as the language of power, even though 60 percent of the population spoke Flemish. To get on in the army, public administration, universities and the law, the Flemish were until recently obliged to speak French.

Duinenbrug, a wooden drawbridge across the Potterierei

In the 19th century, Wallonia grew rich on its coal resources, while Flanders remained largely agricultural. A militant literary movement hailed by Bruges poet-priest Guido Gezelle, helped the Dutch language achieve parity with French in public administration in 1898.

Flemish nationalism reemerged in World War I, when it was exposed that 75 percent of frontline troops were Dutch-speaking and could not understand their officers, 75 percent of whom could not speak Dutch. Thousands died as a result; some Flemings sided with the German occupiers in protest. The Nazis exploited Flemish dissatisfaction in World War II, and won the support of numerous collaborators.

Devolution

A reversal of economic fortunes has led Flanders to achieve greater autonomy. Decline of the coal and steel industries in the south has been countered by growth in the high-tech and port-services sectors in the north. Progressive devolution since the 1970s has given the regions control over economic, social and cultural policy, while tax and foreign policy remain federal competences.

There has been great resentment in Flanders that the thriving local economy is hampered by 'financial transfers' to the south, where former industrial towns are blighted by unemployment. But as any major reform must be passed by at least 50 per cent of French-speakers, the minority community is effectively able to prevent change, a situation criticised as undemocratic by many in Flanders. The far-right Vlaams Belang (Flemish Interest) party won one in four votes across Flanders in 2004 forcing the mainstream parties to form ever wider coalitions and adapt their own policies to demand further devolution. In recent elections however, the more moderate New Flemish Alliance has risen in popularity, seemingly at the expense of their far right counterparts.

PEOPLE

Despite political tensions, most Flemings muddle along happily with their compatriots in day-to-day life. As Belgians they share much common ground: strong family values, a respect for convention and love of material comforts, not to mention a good meal with beer. As many French-speakers as Flemings holiday on the Flemish coast, while many Flemings retire to the Ardennes.

Bruges has none of the students that give Antwerp, Ghent and Brussels their edge, while the Moroccan and Turkish communities that are so visible in other cities are all but absent here. The cultured, slightly older-than-average locals are very polite to the millions of visitors who pass through Bruges, but keep a distance with all but their closest circle.

The Markt, centre of activity in Bruges

TOP TIPS FOR EXPLORING BRUGES AND ITS ENVIRONS

Booking advisable. The restaurants in Bruges are busy year-round and not just in peak seasons. It is therefore advisable to book for evening meals in advance, otherwise you might struggle to find a table on the night. Most will be happy to speak English if you call in advance to reserve a table.

Sales. Sales periods in Belgium are strictly regulated and take place in the months of January and July only. Look out for the magic words *Solden* (Sales) or *Total Uitverkoop* (Everything Must Go). Mark-downs tend to increase during the course of the month, starting at 30 percent and increasing to 70 percent.

Tickets. Tickets for concerts, gigs and other performances are sold at the In&Uit tourist office and box office on 't Zand (daily 10am–6pm or online at www.tickets brugge.be). For an advance overview of what's on, the Cultuurcentrum website (www.ccbrugge.be) is easy to navigate and tickets can be booked online or at tel: 050 44 30 60).

Minnewater toilets. Worth a mention since there are so few public conveniences in Bruges, these are located on the west side of the lake. In all public toilets in Belgium, including in some cafés, you will need spare change to pay the attendant.

Groening Museum Shop. As well as the small shop within the Groeninge, there is a much larger museum shop with a broad array of gift items, such as jewellery, games and bags, located in a former stable block in the Arentshuis courtyard (open Tue–Sun 10am–6pm).

Heavenly sauna. The Hemelhuis (Heaven House; tel: 050 67 96 93; www. hemelhuis.be; Sept–May Thur and Fri 1.30–10.30pm, Sat 12.30–6pm; June–Aug Thur and Fri 5.30– 10.30pm; charge; private hire only on other days) is a beautiful sauna and hammam, where Moorish lamps and mosaics add warmth to the cool post-industrial design. Mixed nudity is the rule, as is typical for saunas in Belgium, but there is a women-only slot on Tuesdays.

Coastal tram. The Coastal Tram (www. dekusttram.be) runs non-stop the length of the Belgian coast, linking De Panne by the French border with Knokke by the Netherlands, and passing through every resort on the way, often just metres behind the beach. Operated by Flemish public transport company De Lijn, the service runs from early morning to late at night, with tickets priced according to length of trip.

Ghent street festival. For a period of 10 days in mid-July, Gentenaars hold one of Europe's largest music, theatre and street festivals, the Ghent Festivities (Gentse Feesten). Centred around St James's Church (Sint-Jacobskerk), events include a reenactment of the Noose Bearers' (Stroppendragers) Procession, recalling the humiliation of rebellious citizens by Charles V in 1540.

Flemish and international fare

FOOD AND DRINK

The Belgians are famous for their mussels, beer, chocolate and fries, but how about North Sea shrimps and Ostend sole, 'Belgian Blue' beef and wild boar? It's a well-used phrase but as true today as ever: everyone eats well in Belgium.

A tradition of medieval banquets and Brueghelian feasts has left its mark on the Belgians, who love nothing better than a hearty, convivial meal with family or friends. Large family groups get together on Sundays and public holidays for a long, lazy lunch stretching far into the afternoon.

Large numbers of tourists mean that eating out in Bruges is more expensive than in other cities, and the high turnover of clientele means that restaurants in prime locations need not fear for their reputation. In addition, with no major student population, there is little demand for dining on a shoestring, so budget options are few and far between.

LOCAL CUISINE

In Flanders, the regional cuisine is dominated by fish and seafood, grilled meats and fresh seasonal vegetables. Brussels is famous for its *stoemp* (mash with vegetables, served with sausage) and meatballs in tomato sauce, while Wallonia has excellent mushrooms, game and wild boar from the Ardennes, cooked in rich, fruity sauces enhanced with beer. Mussels, the nation's favour-

ite food, are in fact imported mostly from the Netherlands. And of course, everyone eats fries.

Typical dishes include a dark beef stew cooked for hours with beer *(Vlaamse stoofkarbonaden/carbonades flamandes)* and *waterzooï*, a Ghent stew of fish or chicken, potatoes, carrots and onion in a thin, creamy sauce. In season from August to April, mussels *(mosselen)* are cooked in a thin stock of celery and onion and served in a large black pot – use an empty shell as a pincer for eating the rest – accompanied by fries and mayonnaise. Game dishes are mainly available in autumn and winter, while Belgian endive wrapped in ham and baked in a white sauce topped with cheese *(gegratineerd witloof)* is another warming winter dish. Shrimp croquettes, a starter of tiny shrimps mixed with béchamel sauce and deep-fried in breadcrumbs, served with a sprig of deep-fried parsley, is a year-round favourite. And every chef has his own recipe for eel in green sauce *(paling in't groen)*, a light dish where the eel is cooked with a herby mixture of chervil, spinach, parsley, sorrel and tarragon and lemon balm.

Classic moules frites   *Tucking into a stew*

Few Belgians are vegetarians, so visiting veggies should avoid Belgian cuisine or they may find themselves stuck with omelettes and vegetable side dishes. Lebanese, Oriental, Indian and some Italian restaurants will offer many tastier options.

WHERE TO EAT

Restaurants

Everyone in Belgium dines out, and there are restaurants to suit all tastes. Neighbourhood establishments – many serving international cuisine such as Greek, Lebanese or Italian – will have paper tablecloths and toothpicks in a plastic pot; the formal variety will serve artful creations inspired by French cuisine, and have a dedicated wine waiter. Chain restaurants are unheard of beyond fast-food outlets; the majority are characterful family-run firms that take pride in serving well-presented, good food. Staff are likely to have followed professional training and can advise on dishes and wines.

Many of the high-end establishments are owned by chefs who have made their name working in the best kitchens in the business, and established enough credibility to stamp their personality on a solo venture, designing a unique menu style. Since the country is so small – and Flanders and Wallonia almost separate countries within themselves – reputations and career history are widely known and discussed by food critics, prompting locals to travel a fair distance for a good restaurant. They are mainly open from noon–2 or 2.30pm and 6.30–10pm.

Brasseries

There is no exact definition for the title, but for our purposes brasseries are open all day for drinks and prioritise tables for diners around mealtimes. Less formal and more lively than a restaurant, they will serve a full, predictable menu of North Sea fish dishes, salads, steaks and classics like Belgian beef stew, chicory *gratin* and rabbit cooked in cherry beer, plus a standard selection of desserts: chocolate mousse, tarte Tatin, crème brûlée and ices. The large majority of tourist-focused restaurants in Bruges are brasseries; several will also serve food outside standard mealtimes (but if they say 'The kitchen is closed,' you will get a microwaved dish).

Bars and cafés

Many bars do basic menus, such as soup, spaghetti Bolognese, omelettes and toasted sandwiches. The cuisine is not fantastic, but is perfectly satisfying for empty bellies. Most cafés serve a complimentary nibble when you buy a round of drinks: a sweet biscuit with a hot drink, peanuts with cold drinks. In addition, many also offer a 'mixed portion' for a few euros – a plate of cheese or salami chunks, served with mustard,

Brugse Zot, a local beer

pickles and celery salt. Shared between 2–4 people these make for a filling snack with a few beers.

Tearooms

Tearooms are a feature of the coast and in Bruges; they are uncommon elsewhere in the country. Targeted squarely at day-trippers, they serve light lunches and afternoon snacks such as waffles, pancakes and ices, mainly with hot or soft drinks, although many also serve alcohol. In Bruges, they also offer a good-value alternative to hotel breakfast, if this is not included in your room price.

DRINKS

Beer

Belgium produces around 500 types of beer, and each brand must be served in its own distinctive glass. There used to be thousands of local breweries – just one survives in Bruges – but few could compete with the Leuven-based

brewer of Stella Artois, Hoegaarden, Leffe and Jupiler. With roots that can be traced back to 1366, it is now the world's no. 1 brewer, renamed AB InBev following a merger with Anheuser-Busch in late 2008.

Beer is served chilled from the tap or the bottle. Typical local varieties include the following:

Lambic beers are wild beers, exposed to wild yeast during fermentation. Gueuze is one type of lambic, which are often quite sour and dry and to which fruit flavours are often added. Kriek is a lambic beer fermented with Morello cherries, giving it its characteristic dark-red hue.

Trappist beers are brewed in an abbey under the control of Trappist monks and are top-fermented ales. Of 171 Trappist monasteries in the world, seven produce beer, six of them in Belgium: Chimay, Orval, Rochefort, Westmalle, Westvleteren and Achelse Kruis.

White beer *(witbier)* is cloudy and often comes with a slice of lemon. Hoegaarden and Brugse Tarwebier are two varieties.

Genever

Belgian gin, increasingly hard to find, is made from distilled grains (usually barley, which gives it more body than English gin), flavoured with juniper berries, caraway seeds or fennel. This was the tipple that 17th-century British troops discovered during the Dutch War of Independence against the Spanish,

---

Food and Drink Prices

Throughout this book, we have used the following price guide for a two-course meal for one, with glass of house wine:

€€€€ = over 100 euros
€€€ = 60–100 euros
€€ = 30–60 euros
€ = below 30 euros

Fresh from the fries van   *Café life on the Markt*

giving them 'Dutch courage'. It comes in three varieties: Oude, the old, straw-coloured, pungently sweet version; Jonge, a younger, more delicately fla-voured variety; and Korenwijn, which is cask-aged with a high percentage of malted spirit.

Mineral water

The hilly Ardennes in southern Belgium has several mineral-water sources. Many of these are bottled for sale, including Spa, Chaudfontaine and Bru. Tap water is perfectly drinkable, but few restaurants will be happy to serve it with a meal.

Tea and coffee

Tea in Belgium is invariably insipid, served as a cup of hot (not boiling) water with a flavourless bag on the side. Fruit-flavoured and herbal teas are widely available, however, and com-monly drunk at the end of a meal in the evening. Fresh mint tea, inspired by the Moroccan community, may be available in trendy places.

Coffee is better: standard coffee *(koffie)* comes in a medium-sized cup and saucer with a dose of creamer on the side; milky coffee *(koffie ver-keerd)* is usually a glass with a dose of espresso and hot milk. Cappuccino is usually made with a dollop of sweet, whipped cream on a black coffee and not frothy milk.

Large coffee chains ubiquitous else-where that serve vats of milky coffee have not yet reached Belgium, with, for example, barely a handful of Starbucks in the country.

Fries van

The fries van *(frietkot)* – usually a fixed caravan – is an institution in every Bel-gian town; perfect for a budget munch on the go, and no calories spared. In Bruges, the *frietkot* has pride of place on the Markt, in front of the Belfry.

Chips are cut thick and fried twice for the unique Belgian consistency – an ini-tial long fry to cook the potato, then a rest, then a hotter flash-fry for the crunchy edge – and served with salt added, wrapped in a paper cornet or on a plastic tray *(bak)*. The server will ask if you want them open – the classic way, to eat stand-ing up by the van – or to take away *(Om mee te nemen)*, wrapped in paper.

Sauces cost about 50 cents extra and include mayonnaise, tartare, ketchup, curry-ketchup, spicy mayo mixes Sam-ourai and Andalousian, and red-hot Pili Pili. You can ask to have the sauce on the side, in a mini plastic tray, for dipping.

The vans also sell soft drinks and a variety of meat accompaniments: meat-ball *(bal)*, meat stick *(fri-candel)*, burger, brochette (wooden skewer with meat and veg).

For the max-out meal, go for a *mitrail-lette* (literally, machine-gun): a long baguette roll filled with a brochette, salad and fries, and lathered with sauce.

Leather bags at Delvaux

SHOPPING

Few visitors leave Bruges without a consignment of chocolate and beer, two products for which Belgium is rightly famed. Other souvenirs may include lace, art books and prints, or hip fashions from a world-renowned designer.

SHOPPING AREAS

Lace, beer and chocolate shops are concentrated in the well-worn groove between the Burg, Markt and Beguinage, along Breidelstraat, Wollestraat, Katelijnestraat and around Walplein. Needless to say, you will not find the best bargains in these areas.

Elsewhere, the main shopping areas are the parallel streets running west from the Markt to the 't Zand: Steenstraat and Geldmuntstraat (which become Zuidzandstraat and Noordzandstraat). Around St Saviour's Cathedral are some good antique stores, while Wollestraat, Sint-Jakobsstraat and Vlamingstraat have stylish interiors stores.

BEER

Bruges has many specialist beer shops, all within easy walking distance of the Markt. These shops are ideal for insider recommendations, hard-to-find varieties and souvenir packs. Two of the best are: Bacchus Cornelius at Academiestraat 17 and De Bier Tempel at Philipstockstraat 7.

If you just want Leffe, Duvel or Chimay, you will get a better price in a supermarket: Carrefour Express (Smedenstraat 62, Katelijnestraat 76, Langerei 17 and Vlamingstraat 2) or Proxy Delhaize (Noordzandstraat 4). If you are driving back to the UK, do not count on buying Belgian beer in Calais's hypermarkets, which mainly stock French pils.

CHOCOLATE

Belgium makes some of the best chocolate in the world – made exclusively with cocoa butter – and is most famous for its pralines: sculpted shells containing various fillings, of which a dizzying variety exist. Every Belgian has their own opinion on who makes the best, and on Saturday afternoons you can see people lining up at chocolatiers to buy a box of mixed pralines, which can be chosen according to preference (no dark; all dark; no alcohol, etc). A box *(ballotin)* of pralines is a common gift to your hosts when you are invited to dinner.

The large chains are reliable and good and are all on Steenstraat: Confiserie Dalipan (cheapest), Neuhaus and Galler. Local makers are numerous, but select wisely: Van Oost (Wollestraat 11), Sweertvaegher (Philipstockstraat 29)

Chocolate logs   *Handmade lace*

and Chocolate Line (Simon Stevinplein 17) are all authentic.

LACE

Once the main local export, lace is still widely promoted in the city. Most items on sale are machine-made in the Far East, but handmade lace, including antique samples, can still be found; most shops sell a mix of the two – and none is correct to claim that they are the only one selling the handmade variety.

Handmade lace is expensive: for a large tablecloth or long wedding veil, count on paying upwards of 400 euros. The shop near the Lace Centre in St Anna, 't Apostelientje (Balstraat 11), is very good, as are Kantuweeltje (Philipstockstraat 11) and Claeys Antique (Katelijnestraat 54).

BOOKS, MUSIC AND ART

Comic strips are Belgium's biggest literary export. De Striep Club at Katelijnestraat 42 is the best address in Bruges for comics, though most bookstores boast a healthy selection of Tintin books and other local comic stars.

The Markt is good for general books, international press, music and multimedia, with several bookstores and the large FNAC department store. Just off the square at Kuipersstraat 1 is Raaklijn, a favourite among book-lovers.

Its musical counterpart, selling a rarefied selection from jazz to Flemish folk, is Rombaux (Mallebergplaats 13). It isn't cheap, but there are listening rooms and the staff are knowledgeable.

Another excellent source of books and gift ideas is the Museum Shop, housed in a former coach house at Dijver 16. It stocks books, cards and posters of works by Flemish Primitives and other Belgian artists, but also art-themed jewellery, watches and bags.

FASHION AND DESIGN

Belgium's fashion design roster is impressive: Ann Demeulemeester, Dries van Noten, Diane von Furstenberg, Martin Margiela and Olivier Theyskens are just some home-grown fashion darlings. Young, Bruges-born Bruno Pieters has been tipped for the top by Suzy Menkes. At the time of writing, his label is only available online (www.honestby.com), though cutting-edge Belgian fashion can be admired at L'Héroïne (Noordzandstraat 32), Essentiel (Noordzandstraat 42) and Olivier Strelli (Eiermarkt 3 for women, Geldmuntstraat 19 for men).

For accessories, Optique Hoet at Vlamingstraat 19 is a local, avant-garde glasses designer. And Delvaux (Breidelstraat 2) is an established Brussels leather goods firm, which does luxurious and classic bags, gloves and jewellery.

Two rustic and romantic homestyle stores also deserve a mention: the Dutch chain Dille & Kamille on Simon Stevinplein 17–18, and adorably romantic Ark van Zarren at Zuidzandstraat 19.

Brugs Beertje is a good choice for beer lovers

ENTERTAINMENT

Bruges is a major player on the Flemish arts scene, with a renowned orchestra and a calendar rich in festivals for jazz, early music, film and dance. Its nightlife is eclectic and unpretentious, ideal for relaxing after a day pounding the cobbles.

Rather like the city itself, Bruges's cultural scene is small but perfectly formed. The modern Concert Hall, historic City Theatre and laid-back festivals attract world-class orchestras, cutting-edge dance companies, experimental music composers and famed jazz artists. The nightlife scene is more restrained, but contains a great selection for somewhere so easy to explore on foot, making the transition easy from cosy beer bar to mini dance club – and not an entrance charge or grumpy doorman in sight.

MUSIC

Classical

Bruges has a strong reputation on the classical music scene, upheld by the large number of concerts held in churches around in the city and the state-of-the-art Concert Hall (Concertgebouw). Large orchestras perform in the 1,300-seat auditorium, while the 300-seat chamber music room – an architectural showpiece with concrete vertical tiers – is ideal for intimate performances.

Fans of early music are especially well served. The Concert Hall's resident orchestra is period-instrument ensemble Anima Eterna, led by renowned harpischordist-pianist-conductor Jos van Immerseel. And the Bruges leg of the Flanders Festival, held each year in late July–early August, is famous for its Musica Antiqua programme, which celebrates modern versions of early music.

Carillon

Wherever you go in Bruges, you are rarely beyond earshot of the 17th-century carillon in the city's Belfry, which is programmed to play a variety of tunes, from Mozart to Jacques Brel, every 15 minutes. The city's carilloneur also performs live concerts which last 45 minutes; these can best be heard from the courtyard of the Cloth Hall.

Contemporary, rock and jazz

The country-wide Ars Musica festival in March and April is a contemporary music bonanza, with several concerts in Bruges, while the Concert Hall programme includes regular avant-garde classical, electronica and jazz events.

The local jazz and rock scene is small-scale compared to bigger cities,

Free concert on the Markt   *A former cinema*

but still manages to attract international artists for intimate gigs. Located just outside the historic centre, the Cactus Musiekcentrum, based primarily in the MaZ venue just west of the station, features upcoming indie bands as well as established figures on the world and folk circuit. It also organises the summertime Cactus Music Festival in the Minnewater Park. De Werf in the north of the city is the go-to address for jazz.

THEATRE AND DANCE

The 19th-century City Theatre (Stadsschouwburg) on Vlamingstraat is the hub of a network of cultural venues around the city, and programmes an exciting selection of Dutch-language theatre, dance, music and literature events.

Belgium's principal classical dance troupe – the Antwerp-based Royal Ballet of Flanders – brings its touring productions to the Concert Hall several times a year. Its repertoire focuses on ballet classics, but productions are far from staid: the company frequently works with contemporary artists to create ambitious staging and set design.

Contemporary dance is one of Belgium's most successful cultural exports, thanks largely to Flemish companies, many of which use live music to thrilling effect in ambitious productions. Dance has a strong local following, and the City Theatre and Concert Hall feature local and international companies with a regularity unusual in a small town.

FILM

One advantage of Dutch being spoken by little over 20 million people is that bar animation and kids' movies, films are screened in their original version, subtitled. The Lumière Cinema on Sint-Jakobsstraat shows everything from Hollywood mainstream to foreign arthouse movies. The Kinepolis multiplex, 5km (3 miles) south of the centre, has a larger choice. Each year Bruges hosts the MOOOV Festival in April and the quirky Razor Reel Fantastic Film Festival at the end of October.

NIGHTLIFE

Bruges has a fairly demure nightlife. Locals tend to prefer a quiet drink with friends at bohemian venues such as Lokkedize or De Republiek; jazz or blues in wine bars like Wijnbar Est or Vino Vino; or a late drink after a concert in the Concert Hall café. Beer fans meet at 't Brugs Beertje and De Garre. Few bars in Bruges stay open really late, but those that do – including several small venues that have dance floors – are concentrated around Kraanplein, Eiermarkt and 't Zand, the last aimed more at a teeny-bopper brigade. Club nights are organised on an ad hoc basis, usually in out-of-town venues. Check bars for flyers.

Van Eyck's 'Madonna and Child with Canon Joris van der Paele' (1436)

HISTORY: KEY DATES

The people of Bruges have lived through invasion and occupation since records began, with fertile Flanders a favourite battleground of warring nations. Below are the key historical events that shaped the city.

EARLY PERIOD TO THE MIDDLE AGES

1stC BC	Celtic farmers are set up on the coastal plain by what is now Bruges.
1stC AD	A Gallo-Roman settlement is founded beside the rivers Reie and Dijver, and maintains trading links with Britain and Gaul.
862	Baldwin I is the first count of Flanders and occupies the Burg castle.
c.1040	An English text calls Bruges an important maritime trading centre, but by the end of the century access to the sea is closed by silting.
1134	A canal is built from Bruges to Damme, reopening a maritime trading route.
1250	With 40–50,000 citizens, Bruges is a large and rich city.
1297	King Philip IV of France annexes Flanders.
1302	French citizens and sympathisers are massacred in the 'Bruges Matins'. An army of Flemish peasants and craftsmen slaughter French knights at the Battle of the Golden Spurs at Kortrijk.

BURGUNDIAN RULE TO THE ENLIGHTENMENT

1384	Count Louis is succeeded by his daughter Margaret, wife of Philip the Bold, duke of Burgundy. The dazzling Burgundian century begins.
15thC	Cloth-making declines, but trade and banking still prosper.
1477	Duke Charles the Bold dies, succeeded by his daughter, Mary of Burgundy, wife of Habsburg Crown Prince Maximilian of Austria.
1482	After Mary's death, the Habsburg reign begins.
1520	The Zwin's silting closes Bruges's sea access. Economic decline begins.
1566	Protestant 'Iconoclasts' sack churches across the Low Countries.

Signing the Treaty of Utrecht in 1715

1580	The city signs the Treaty of Utrecht against Spain; Protestantism becomes the only permitted religion.
1584	Spain re-establishes control. Many Protestants flee to Holland.
1622	Opening of a canal to Ostend gives Bruges a new outlet to the sea.
1715	By the Treaty of Utrecht, Belgium passes under the authority of the Austrian Holy Roman Emperor Charles VI.
1744–8	Bruges is occupied by the French.
1753	Coupure Canal opens, allowing sea-going vessels into city centre.
1794–5	Revolutionary France invades.
1815	Napoleon defeated at Waterloo. Bruges becomes part of the Kingdom of the Netherlands under William I of Orange.

MODERN ERA

1830	Southern Netherlands revolt against Dutch rule, resulting in the formation of the Kingdom of Belgium.
1847	Hunger riots erupt in Bruges, the poorest city in Belgium.
1904	Work on the new Bruges sea harbour, Zeebrugge, is completed.
1914–18	World War I. Battles around Ypres (Ieper) are among the war's bloodiest. Germans destroy Zeebrugge harbour when they leave.
1940–4	World War II. Germans occupy Belgium.

POST-WAR, EUROPE AND FEDERALISATION

1948	Customs union between Belgium, the Netherlands and Luxembourg (Benelux).
1957	Belgium is a founder member of the European Economic Community, the forerunner of today's European Union.
1980	Establishment of Flanders and Wallonia as federal regions and of the Flemish, French and German-speaking language communities.
2002	Bruges is European City of Culture for a year. The euro replaces the Belgian franc as unit of currency.
2011	A new Belgian government is formed after bitter negotiations between Flemish and Walloon parties lasting more than 500 days during which the country was left without a formal government – a new world record.
2013	Philippe of Belgium ascends to the throne following the abdication of his father, Albert II, for health reasons.

BEST ROUTES

Bruges crest in the Burg

CITY HIGHLIGHTS

Prepare to pound the cobbles: this is a whistle-stop tour of the city's stellar sights, and packs the wow factor at every turn. Keep an eye out for cyclists, horse-drawn carriages and tourists looking every way except forwards.

> **DISTANCE:** 3.5km (2.25 miles)
> **TIME:** 3 hours
> **START:** Markt
> **END:** Concert Hall, 't Zand
> **POINTS TO NOTE:** Opening hours are not an issue here (bar the Beguinage: 6.30am–6.30pm), so this is the perfect Monday walk, when museums are shut.

This circuit of the city's landmarks is ideal for a first or fleeting visit. The other routes in this book (cross-referenced here) explore the sights more fully.

MARKT

Start on the **Markt ①** (Market Square), the heart of daily life in the city past and present (see route 4). The power and freedoms won by the citizens of the medieval town are embodied in the towering **Belfry** (Belfort), built in 1280–1350 and one of the city's three great towers (see route 2). Note: few cafés here offer value for money; if you want to admire the view, order a drink at most.

BURG

Take Breidelstraat at the southeastern corner of the Markt towards the Burg. On the way, note the narrow doorway in the wall that is ancient alley De Garre. There's a lovely pub here, **Staminée de Garre**, see ①, to note for later.

Smaller and more sedate than the Markt – with only a couple of cafés, such as **Tom Pouce** and **Delaney's**, see ② and ③ – the **Burg ②** is the cradle of Bruges, named after the fortified castle that founded the city (see route 3).

Many exceptional monuments and museums are located around the square, from the 13th-century **City Hall** to the **Basilica of the Holy Blood**.

JAN VAN EYCKPLEIN

Leave the Burg by the north, turn right on Philipstockstraat, then left on Wappenmakersstraat. Head north, crossing Sint-Jansplein to reach **Jan van Eyckplein ③**, with historic buildings that recall Bruges's trading heyday in the 11th–13th centuries (see route 8).

Jan van Eyck statue   *The fish market near Groenerei*

Return to the Burg via Kraanrei and Kraanplein (names that recall the crane used to unload goods from incoming barges), the narrow Ieperstraat and Cordoeaniersstraat, then turn left on Philipstockstraat and right back into the Burg.

GROENEREI

Cross over to the narrow **Blinde Ezelstraat ④** (Blind Donkey Street), passing under the arch to reach the canal. The view from the bridge explains why this stretch of canal is called **Groenerei** (Green Canal; see route 7).

Ahead is the colonnaded **Fish Market** (Vismarkt); from Tuesday to Saturday, stallholders sell fish fresh from the North Sea, 10km (6 miles) away at Zeebrugge. To the right is one of several **jetties ⑤** for the departure of canal boat tours. The boats all take the same route and leave many stretches of water clear. Walking around town, you will catch glimpses of narrow waterways overhung with trees and flanked with small gardens. There were once more waterways in the centre – many have been vaulted over.

TANNERS' SQUARE

Turn right into the **Huidenvettersplein** (Tanners' Square; see route 7), with the former **Tanners' Guildhouse ⑥** (1630–1)

Groeninge Museum exhibit

at nos 11–12. After the tanners upped sticks, it became a freshwater fish market. Now it is lined with restaurants. Cross the square to **Rozenhoedkaai** ❼ (Rosary Quay), a quayside with the most stunning vista.

The **mansion** ❽ across the water on the bend in the canal was occupied by 16th-century Spanish magistrate Juan Pérez de Malvenda. During religious troubles from 1578–84, the relic of the Holy Blood was stored here for safekeeping. Continue walking west, keeping the bridge to your right.

DIJVER

Follow **Dijver** (see route 4) to reach the main city art museum: the **Groeninge** ❾. Many of the world-class paintings in here have never left the city. From the garden leading to the museum, turn right to cross Groeninge lane and pass through the courtyard of the **Arentshuis** ❿ museum. Walk diagonally to the left to cross the **Bonifacius footbridge** ⓫. To the right is the 15th-century **Palace of the Lords of Gruuthuse**, a showcase of daily life from the 15th to 19th centuries.

MARIASTRAAT

The footpath brings you out behind the **Church of Our Lady** ⓬ (Onze-Lieve-Vrouwekerk; see route 2), an awe-inspiring monument from the exterior and packed with treasures inside. As you emerge onto Mariastraat, the **Hospital Museum**

– **Memling in St John's** ⓭ (see route 5) is across the road. Founded in the 12th century and a functioning hospital until 1976, it contains several priceless paintings by Hans Memling.

Turn left to cross the bridge. Just after, on the right, a gate in the wall leads to the secluded garden of the **Spanoghe Almshouse** ⓮, one of many historic almshouses dotted around the city, built by trade corporations or wealthy families for the poor and elderly. Visitors are welcome to enter their gardens but are asked to respect the quiet atmosphere.

WALPLEIN

Return to Mariastraat and take the next tiny lane to the right, Stoofstraat, said to be the narrowest street in Bruges, with a good lunch spot, **Malesherbes**, see ❹. The lane brings you to **Walplein** ⓯ (see route 5), site of the sole surviving brewery in Bruges, the **Half Moon Brewery**. Cross the square to Wijngaardstraat. Turn right – or swerve left for the lovely tearoom, **Carpe Diem**, see ❺. On arriving at the junction with the horse drinking fountain, turn right across the bridge for one of Bruges's best-loved sights.

BEGUINAGE

An otherwordly calm pervades the courtyard of the **Beguinage** ⓰ (Begijnhof; see route 5), formerly home to a community of beguines – pious women who did not take the full vows of a nun. Enjoy the tran-

Church of Our Lady   *The famous Half Moon Brewery sign*

quillity of the walled enclosure: proof that even in a tiny city packed with tourists it is still possible to escape the bustle.

Pass the church and leave at the opposite side, turning left to exit the compound. You are now in the **Minnewater Park**, with its lovely lake.

ST SAVIOUR'S CATHEDRAL

Turn right twice, into Professor Doctor Joseph Sebrechtsstraat, passing the **Minnewaterkliniek** ⑰ (1908), a former city hospital and now a retirement home. Turn right at the end, on Oost-meers. This street of terraced houses is a typical snapshot of everyday Bruges. Continue to the end, then wander on a few tiny backstreets to emerge at the rear of **St Saviour's Cathedral** ⑱ (Sint-Salvatorskathedraal; see route 2).

'T ZAND

Turn left on the shopping street Zuidzandstraat, which ends at **'t Zand** (see route 11), the square that is home to the **Concert Hall** ⑲ (Concertgebouw). The walk ends here, close to cafés and the **In&Uit Tourist Office** inside the Concert Hall.

Food and Drink

❶ STAMINÉE DE GARRE

De Garre 1; tel: 050 34 10 29; Mon–Thur noon–midnight, Fri noon–1am, Sat 11.30am–1am, Sun noon–midnight; €
The house brew, Tripel de Garre (10.5 percent), is wisely restricted to three glasses per person at this historic tavern.

❷ TOM POUCE

Burg 17; tel: 050 33 03 36; www.restaurant-tompouce.be; daily 9am–11pm; €
Fish and Flemish cuisine dominate the menu at this restaurant with an unrivalled location. Order a waffle or pancake, sit on the heated terrace and watch the world go by.

❸ DELANEY'S

Burg 8; tel: 050 34 91 45; www.delaneys.be; daily from 10.30am; €€
A popular, friendly Irish pub/restaurant on the Burg, serving Irish and international fare.

❹ MALESHERBES

Stoofstraat 3–5; tel: 050 33 69 24; Wed–Sun noon–1.45pm, 7–9pm; €
This tucked-away eatery serves French food in an informal atmosphere. The front deli opens earlier – at 10am.

❺ CARPE DIEM

Wijngaardstraat 8; tel: 050 33 54 47; www.tearoom-carpediem.be; Wed–Mon 7am–6.30pm; €
Wood panelling and stained glass make the perfect accompaniments to an 'olde-worlde' experience in the tearoom adjoining the Detavernier patisserie and bakery. Civilised without being over-smart.

Two of the three towers: the Belfry and St Saviour's

THE THREE TOWERS

Visible for miles across the flat polder landscape, the towers of the Belfry, St Saviour's Cathedral and the Church of Our Lady compete for dominance of the skyline. This route joins the dots between the towering trio.

DISTANCE: 0.75km (0.5 miles)
TIME: 2.5 hours
START: Belfry
END: Church of Our Lady
POINTS TO NOTE: This walk is best done in the afternoon, Tue–Fri or Sun, when all the sights are open. It can also be followed by route 5, or preceded by it if both are done in reverse.

Like three giants parading in a Flemish folkloric parade, the octagonal tower of the Belfry, square tower of St Saviour's and pinnacle of the Church of Our Lady stalk the skyline of Bruges. Get to know their silhouettes and, wherever you are in the city, you will never be without an orientation point. This short walk introduces these three main players on the Bruges scene; their surroundings feature in later routes.

BELFRY

The great **Belfry** ❶ (Belfort; Markt 7; www.museabrugge.be; daily 9.30am–5pm; charge) dominates the Markt and has long been the symbol of Bruges's civic pride, built between 1280 and 1350 after its wooden predecessor was destroyed by fire.

Its upper section, an octagonal tower, was added in 1486, and leans slightly to the southeast, by a total of 1.2m (4ft) at its summit. A wooden spire that originally topped the tower was destroyed by lightning in 1493, and its replacement by fire in 1741. Today, it stands 83m (51ft) high.

At its base cluster the former **Market Halls** (Hallen), a commercial centre in use since the 13th century, now used for cultural events. In summer, bench seating is provided in the courtyard for audiences of carillon concerts.

The climb

The only one of the three towers open to climb, the Belfry is 366 steps up, and not for the faint-hearted. On the way up is the treasury, where the magistrate's papers, town seal and charter were kept behind iron grilles (1292), which required nine keys to open

Detail from the reliquary of Charles the Good

them. These were held by the burgo-master (mayor) and eight trade-guild leaders, so could not be opened without the assent of all.

Further up is the 6-tonne great bell, and above that the 47-piece carillon, which peals every quarter-hour, controlled mechanically by the rotating metal drum, or, if you are lucky, by the city's own bell-ringer, who sits in a little room and plays concerts to the square. You are rewarded at the top with a 360-degree view, best in the early morning or late afternoon, of this compact city, reduced to a toy-town below.

ST SAVIOUR'S CATHEDRAL

From the Markt take Steenstraat west. As the street changes into Zuidzand-straat, you reach **St Saviour's Cathedral ❷** (Sint-Salvatorskathedraal; www. sintsalvator.be; Mon–Fri 10am–1pm and 2–5.30pm, Sat 10am–1pm and 2–3.30pm, Sun 11–noon and 2–5pm), the oldest parish church in Bruges. It was founded in the 9th century, but only became a cathedral in 1834 after St Donatian's, on the Burg, was destroyed. It is an unusual example of Scheldt Gothic architecture, built mainly in the 12th–15th century, but with a neo-Romanesque brick belfry, which stands 99m (60ft) tall.

Interior

Inside are tapestries, paintings and a Baroque rood-screen topped by a monumental statue of *God the Father* by Artus Quellin the Younger. Look under the late-Gothic choir stalls at the carved misericords (1430), and above the stalls at the coats of arms of the Knights of the Golden Fleece, who assembled here in 1478 in order to elect a new leader. Their choice, Maximilian of Austria, conferred the

Detail from the frescoed tombs, Church of Our Lady

title from the house of Burgundy to the Habsburgs.

In the ambulatory, the first chapel clockwise contains the reliquary of Charles the Good, count of Flanders, who was killed in St Donatian's in 1127. A floor tile allegedly soaked with his blood was brought here and is said to provoke miracles when touched.

Treasury Museum

The cathedral's **Treasury Museum** (Sun–Fri 2–5pm; charge) in the southern transept contains the gory but splendid *Martyrdom of Saint Hippolytus* altarpiece, with the saint being torn limb from limb by four wild horses. The work is attributed to Dirk Bouts (1415–75), with one panel by Hugo van der Goes. Other paintings are by Renaissance artists Pieter Pourbus and Adriaen Ysenbrandt. As well as brass tomb-plates, reliquaries and valuable church plate, a collection of liturgical garments includes a piece of tunic that allegedly belonged to St Bridget of Ireland (*d*.525).

Dining options near the cathedral include **Cafedraal**, **Kardinaalshof** and **Patrick Devos 'De Zilveren Pauw'**, see ①, ② and ③.

CHURCH OF OUR LADY

From the rear of the cathedral, take the narrow Heilige-Geeststraat southeast to the third of the city's beacons, and the tallest of the three: the **Church of Our Lady** ③ (Onze-Lieve-Vrouwekerk; Mari-

astraat; www.museabrugge.be; Mon–Sat 9.30am–5pm, Sun 1.30–5pm; charge), a formidable sight with a 122m (400ft) brick spire. Built between 1290 and 1549, the church is a hotch-potch of different styles.

The church's most valuable treasures, however, are its artworks. Chief among them is a white marble *Madonna and Child* (1506) by Michelangelo, the first work of art to represent the Christ child as an independent person. The Madonna is a subdued, preoccupied figure, while the infant leans nonchalantly on her knee.

The statue is notable for having left Italy, albeit rather by accident. It was sold to Flemish merchant Jan Mouscron after the Italian family who commissioned it for Siena cathedral failed to pay the artist. Its stay in Bruges has not been undisturbed: although Walpole's bid to buy it for England in the 18th century failed, the French whisked it away to Paris during the French Revolution, and the Germans swiped it again in World War II.

Church museum

The choir, chancel and ambulatory comprise the **museum** section of the church (times as church, except closed Mon; charge), where the highlight is the side-by-side tombs of Charles the Bold and his daughter Mary of Burgundy.

Whether their bodies are contained within is a matter of dispute. Charles died in battle in Nancy in 1477 and it

Tomb of Mary of Burgundy, Church of Our Lady

was difficult to identify the body. Mary (who died in a riding accident aged 25, bringing to a close the 100-year reign of the house of Burgundy) may be buried in a set of frescoed tombs discovered beneath the choir in 1979 (now revealed). Either way, their sarcophagi, richly decorated in copper-gilt gold, red and blue, make for an interesting comparative study of late-Gothic and Renaissance carving: Mary's dates from 1502 and is fine and ornate; her father's from some 50 years later has far less detail.

Look up from Mary's tomb to the windows in the nearby wall. This is the 15th-century oratory of the adjoining Palace of the Lords of Gruuthuse, whose wealthy residents could peer down into the church rather than attending mass with the rabble.

Notable paintings include works by Flemish Primitives Dirk Bouts and Hugo van der Goes, and a *Transfiguration* by Gerard David (c.1460–1523), the movement's last painter. Pieter Pourbus (1523–84) recalls the style of the earlier masters in *Last Supper* and *Adoration of the Shepherds*, while Anthony van Dyck's starkly atmospheric *Christ on the Cross* is evocative of Rubens's Antwerp school, where the master described van Dyck as 'the best of my pupils'.

If you are in need of some hearty Flemish fare on exiting the church, make your way to **Marieke Van Brugghe**, see ❹.

Food and Drink

❶ CAFEDRAAL
Zilverstraat 38; tel: 050 34 08 45; www.cafedraal.be; Mon–Sat noon–3pm, 6–11pm; €€€
Just off Zuidzandstraat, a fine collection of 15th-century buildings contains this fashionable eatery specialising in seafood. Open for drinks only from 3–6pm.

❷ KARDINAALSHOF
Sint-Salvatorskerkhof 14; tel: 050 34 16 91; www.kardinaalshof.be; Fri–Tue noon–2.15pm, 7–9.15pm, Thur 7–9.15pm; €€€
A smart townhouse located behind the cathedral is home to this 'special occasion' favourite, where the fixed monthly menus focus on seafood.

❸ PATRICK DEVOS 'DE ZILVEREN PAUW'
Zilverstraat 41; tel: 050 33 55 66; www.patrickdevos.be; Mon–Fri noon–1.30pm, 7–9pm, closed Wed D and Sat L; €€€€
Star chef and wine taster Devos offers a menu that draws on fresh regional produce, complemented by top-class wines at the 'Silver Peacock'.

❹ MARIEKE VAN BRUGGHE
Mariastraat 17; tel: 050 34 33 66; www.mvb.be; daily 11am–9pm, except hols; €€
Despite this restaurant-brasserie-tearoom's touristy location, the locals love its traditional Flemish fare.

City Hall

AROUND THE BURG

Seat of rulers and place of pilgrimage, the cobbled Burg has been the heart of civic and sacred Bruges for over a millennium. This short route explores the historic square and its close surrounds.

DISTANCE: 0.75km (0.5 miles)
TIME: 3 hours
START: Burg
END: St Walburga's Church
POINTS TO NOTE: A good route for a Monday, when many museums and other attractions elsewhere in the city are closed, but all those recommended here are open. To see the relic of the Holy Blood, time your visit to arrive at the Basilica during hours when it is presented to the public for veneration: Apr–Sept daily 11.30am–noon, 2–4pm, Oct–Mar daily 11.30am–noon, Mon, Tue, Thur 2–3pm, Fri–Sun 2–4pm. This route could be followed by No. 6.

The Burg takes its name from the town's first recorded structure: a castle on the site dating from the mid-9th century, when the Franks built a moated fort, or *burcht*, to protect against Viking marauders. This was replaced in the 11th century with a wooden residence, built for the counts of Flanders. By the Burgundian era, the city's rulers were ready for more luxurious quarters, and quit the Burg in the late 14th century for the Prinsenhof across town (see page 69).

You can stand on the Burg and survey all the architectural styles that have marked the city: Romanesque, Gothic, Renaissance, Baroque and neoclassical, right up to the 21st-century steel walkway created by Toyo Ito in 2002, all within a few short paces of each other. Several of the buildings merit closer inspection, although none requires a long visit.

CITY HALL

Pride of place on the Burg goes to the three-turreted **City Hall ❶** (Stadhuis) at No. 12. The late 14th-century building is a masterpiece of Flamboyant Gothic, resplendent with detail. Once highly coloured, it is adorned with the coats of arms of local towns and villages and 34 statues (mostly copies of the originals, destroyed in the 1790s by sympathisers of Revolutionary France) represent-

View of the Old Recorder's House and City Hall

ing saints, prophets and local noblemen and women.

Still mainly used for council business, only the first floor is open to the public. The **City Hall Museum** (Brugge museum Stadhuis; www.museabrugge.be; daily 9.30am–5pm; charge) tells the story of the struggle for power in the city, between aristocrats, councillors and the population. The magnificent **Gothic Hall** has a superb polychrome, rib-vaulted ceiling and is decorated with flamboyant 19th-century biblical murals.

In the adjacent **Maritime Chamber**, historic maps and engravings provide a fascinating history of the town's development. The 1562 engraving by Marcus Gerards, the earliest surviving map of the city, suggests that he must have climbed all the tall buildings in the city to get his bird's-eye view.

BASILICA OF THE HOLY BLOOD

One of the most visited sites in Bruges is tucked in the corner of the Burg at No. 10. The **Basilica of the Holy Blood** ❷ (Heilig-Bloedbasiliek; www.holyblood.com; Apr–Sept daily 9.30am–noon, 2–5pm, Oct–Mar Thur–Tue 10am–noon, 2–5pm) comprises two chapels, one on top of the other. On the ground floor is the Romanesque **St Basil's Chapel**, built 1134–57 as the church of the long-demolished Castle of the Counts, the original residence of the counts of Flanders. The sim-

ple decor and sparse ornamentation stand in direct contrast to the **upper chapel**, which is reached from outside, via a broad spiral staircase behind a three-arched facade, completed in 1534. Built in the 15th century, the chapel has been spoiled somewhat by the over-eager 19th-century decoration and murals, but is still impressive nonetheless. The ceiling looks like an upturned boat, while the bronze pulpit (1728) resembles a cored and stuffed tomato. The relic of the Holy Blood is preserved in a side chapel.

Story of the relic

The relic of the Holy Blood has attracted pilgrims to Bruges for over eight cen-

Old Recorder's House

The colourful house on the Burg between the City Hall and the Liberty of Bruges Palace is the Old Recorder's House (Oude Griffie), built 1534–7. Redecorated in authentic bright colours typical of the period, the building is an example of the Flemish Renaissance style. The bas relief at the top of the facade depicts the ancient Persian legend of a corrupt judge being skinned alive, a popular cautionary tale for lawmakers in medieval times (a 15th-century painting on the same theme hangs in the Groeninge Museum, see page 43). Today the building is occupied by law courts and is not open to the public.

The upper chapel in the Basilica

turies. It consists of a phial containing what is said to be Christ's blood, washed from his body after the Crucifixion by Joseph of Arimathea. Derrick of Alsace, count of Flanders, reportedly brought the relic back from Jerusalem in 1149, having received it in recognition of his heroism during the Second Crusade.

Encased in a silver and rock-crystal phial, it is displayed to the public each afternoon (except Wed) for veneration (for which an offering is encouraged). Many people take the opportunity to kiss it.

Basilica Museum

A side door beside the entrance to the upper chapel leads into the **Basilica Museum** (same opening times as church; charge), two rooms containing some fascinating articles, not least a reliquary (1617) made with 30kg (66lbs) of gold and silver and over 100 precious stones.

A manuscript details the ceremonial garments worn by the Noble Brotherhood of the Holy Blood, which inspires participants in the annual procession today, and a 1556 painting by Pieter Pourbus showing the Brotherhood's 31 mem-

bers. Other treasures include a tiny silver crown with gems that belonged to Mary of Burgundy (1457–82), which is especially dainty.

LIBERTY OF BRUGES PALACE

In the southeastern corner of the Burg stands the **Liberty of Bruges Palace** ❸ (Landhuis van het Brugse Vrije), a building dating from the early 18th century. The Liberty of Bruges was an autonomous administrative district of towns and villages outside the city, important enough to be represented from 1127 alongside Bruges, Ghent and Ypres at the Flemish Estates (a kind of early parliament). Its aldermen met in a Palace on this site from

Liberty of Bruges Palace   *Old Recorder's House*

the 14th century (much of the surviving building dates from a rebuild in 1722–7).

In 1794, the Liberty was disbanded by Revolutionary France, and the palace later became the law court. Since 1988, it has been used for municipal offices.

Renaissance Hall

One early part of the building survives: the chamber where the Liberty of Bruges aldermen met, known as the **Renaissance Hall** (Renaissancezaal; www.museabrugge.be; 9.30am–12.30pm, 1.30–5pm; charge). The building, which can be visited daily, has been restored to its original condition and is one of 16 historical sights that form the municipal Bruges Museum (Bruggemuseum) network – the sights in this group may be visited using the good-value combined museum pass available from the Tourist Office.

The hall contains one of the most notable artworks in the whole city: a black marble fireplace and carved oak chimney-piece covering an entire wall, created in 1528–31 by Lanceloot Blondeel as a tribute to Charles V. The carving celebrates the imperial army's victory over Francis I of France at Pavia in 1525; the Treaty of Madrid, which was signed the following year, would free Belgium from French domination. The craftsmanship of the ensemble is truly staggering, but the brass handholds for the rural noblemen to use while drying their boots at the fire are the sort of domestic touch that everyone remembers.

TOYO ITO PAVILION AND ST DONATIAN'S

Head to the north of the square. The city's earliest known religious foundation – and original cathedral – stood on the tree-lined area where the modern **Toyo Ito Pavilion** ❹ (Paviljoen Toyo Ito) is situated today. Japanese architect Ito created the pavilion on the Burg to mark Bruges's year as European Capital of Culture in 2002. The open walkway occupies the site of the former central chapel in the destroyed St Donatian's Cathedral, and symbolises the link between the Bruges of yesterday and today.

St Donatian's, begun around 940 and a cathedral from 1562, was destroyed in 1799–1802 by supporters of the French Revolution. In 1127, Charles the Good, count of Flanders, was murdered in the church for defending the poor against abuse by wealthy grain-hoarders.

It was a major cultural institution in medieval times, with a great library, music school and scriptorium, where illuminated manuscripts were produced. Bookshops were clustered around the cathedral and attracted pioneers of the trade: William Caxton produced the first printed book in the English language in Bruges in 1473, a *Recuyell of the Histories of Troy* ordered

Treats at Choco–Story

by Margaret of York, duchess of Burgundy, before he left to introduce printing in England.

The excavated choir of the church can be explored (free; enquire at reception) in the basement of the Crowne Plaza hotel on the corner of the square.

REFRESHMENT OPTIONS

Now leave the Burg to the north and then turn right on Philipstockstraat, where there are two good choices for eating: the successful **Het Dagelijks Brood**

chain for hot drinks, snacks and light lunches at No. 21, see ❶, or, for a more substantial meal, **Baobab**, at No. 27, see ❷. Take the first left into Wappenmakersstraat, where there is yet another good lunch stop, the healthy-eating **Lotus**, see ❸.

CHOCOLATE MUSEUM

Wappenmakersstraat leads to Sint-Jansplein (St John's Square). A medieval building standing on the northeastern corner of the square at No. 2 Wijnzakstraat, the **Huis de Croon** is home to a privately run museum of chocolate, **Choco-Story** ❺ (www.choco-story.be; daily 10am–5pm; charge), a popular visit indeed though perhaps not one to be prioritised over the city's historic sights.

The museum tells the story of the cocoa bean, from its use as currency by Aztec and Maya civilisations to chocolate's status as a hot drink favoured by European royalty. Full of information and artefacts – ancient manuscripts, porcelain, chocolate sculptures – but rather lacking in interactive features to keep children entertained, the visit concludes with demonstrations of chocolate-making and a tasting session.

ST WALBURGA'S CHURCH

Pass down the side of Choco-Story along Sint-Jansstraat, turn right at the

Holy Blood Procession

The relic of the Holy Blood has been worshipped in Bruges for over seven centuries: in the past, it was said that the dried blood turned to liquid at regular intervals, a phenomenon declared to be a miracle by Pope Clement V (1264–1314).

On Ascension Day every year, the relic is carried through Bruges in the famous Procession of the Holy Blood (Heilig-Bloed Processie), the most important of West Flanders's festivals, featuring 1,500 participants acting out biblical scenes, watched by 50,000 pilgrims and spectators. The bishop of Bruges himself transports the relic in an ornate gold-and-silver reliquary that is kept for the rest of the year in the chapel's museum.

The cool interior of St Walburga's Church

end and then left along Korte Ridder-straat. This brings you to the front of **St Walburga's Church** ❻ (Sint-Walburgakerk; daily 10am–noon and 2–5pm), a Baroque oratory which was erected by a Jesuit community from 1619 until 1642.

Inside the church

The cool interior is flooded with silvery light, which bounces off the riot of marble within, from the black-and-white floor tiles to the three altars and, best of all, an intricately carved Carrara marble altar-rail. A fabulously over-the-top oak pulpit (1669) competes for the wow-factor, with its double staircase and scalloped canopy upheld by trumpeting angels.

Rather more discreet is a triptych with an unusual theme: *Our Lady of the Dry Tree* (1620), by Pieter Claeissens the Younger, shows the Virgin and Child perched in the branches of a tree appearing to Philip the Good, duke of Burgundy, as he prays on the eve of battle for victory against the French.

Food and Drink

❶ HET DAGELIJKS BROOD

Philipstockstraat 21; tel: 050 33 60 50; www.painquotidien.com; Wed–Mon 8am–6.30pm; €
Local branch of the hit Belgian bakery and café (known as Le Pain Quotidien in French-speaking parts and abroad), which has franchised its scrubbed pine communal table philosophy to cities around the world. Wholesome bread, dangerously addictive chocolate spreads and tarts, and generous breakfasts, but the tasty open sandwiches are not for larger appetites.

❷ BAOBAB

Philipstockstraat 27; tel: 050 33 14 08; www.bistro-baobab.be; Fri–Wed noon–2pm, 6.30–10.30pm, except Sat lunch and Wed dinner closed; €€
This cheerful South African bistro uses spices, coconut milk and other flavours of sunnier climes, washed down, as you would expect, with wines of the region. The meat (springbok, ostrich) and fish (tilapia, tiger prawns) are imported direct from South Africa, and there are plenty of veggie options too. Gluten or lactose intolerance can also be catered for, on request.

❸ LOTUS

Wappenmakersstraat 5; tel: 050 33 10 78; www.lotus-brugge.be; Mon–Sat 11.45am–2pm; €
This long-established mainly vegetarian restaurant serves lunches only and is very popular with locals. It offers good-value, health-focused dishes, and caters for carnivores with either organic lamb moussaka or lamb stew.

Restaurants on the Markt

MARKT TO THE MUSEUMS

The trading wealth of medieval Bruges found expression in a new painting technique that changed the course of Western art. Follow this route from the city's commercial nerve centre to its museums along the Dijver.

DISTANCE: 0.75km (0.5 miles), not including distance walked in the museums
TIME: A half day
START: Markt
END: Gruuthuse Museum
POINTS TO NOTE: The museums in this route are closed every Monday (apart from Easter Monday and Whit Monday). This route can be combined with either No. 5 or with No. 2 conducted in reverse, starting at the Church of Our Lady.

The hub of daily life in Bruges for over 1,000 years, the Markt is the unrivalled epicentre of activity in the city. Buses, cyclists and horse-drawn carriages rattle across the cobbles, dodging tourists as they gaze skywards at the Belfry or make a carb-crazed beeline for the fries van (see page 17). A southern detour to the Dijver will not take you away from the tourists, but does guarantee a succession of aesthetic treats: from the Flemish Primitives in the Groeninge to the turreted Gruuthuse, a 15th-century family mansion and repository of decorative and applied arts.

MARKT

The **Markt** ❶ (Market Square) has been the hub of commercial life in the city since the 10th century, home to a market since 958; one is still held every Wednesday. In contrast with the nearby Burg (see page 34), which was the historic centre of government and Church, activities on the Markt have always centred around trade, as well as the odd jousting tournament or parade.

Market Halls
The southern edge of the square is dominated by the vast Belfry (see page 30) and **Market Halls** ❷ (Hallen), built around a central courtyard. These were the pride of the city for three centuries, a meeting place for traders from partner cities in the Hanseatic League. The existing structure was built in the 13th–15th centuries to replace its

Provincial House

The city's coat of arms

wooden predecessor, and is used today as a shopping and exhibition centre.

Provincial House

A canal now curtailed to the north, near Kraanplein, used to flow into the east side of the Markt, where a vast **Water Hall** (Waterhalle) straddled the canal, with broad quaysides for unloading goods from small barges. The neo-Gothic **Provincial House ❸** (Provinciaal Hof; closed to the public), seat of the provincial governor of West Flanders, was built on the site in 1887–92. Next door is the **central post office** (Mon–Fri 9am–6pm, Sat 9am–3pm). **Historium** (www.historium.be; daily 10am-6pm; charge), on the other side of the Provincial House, brings Bruges' Golden Age to life though film, sounds, smells and special effects.

Guildhouses and mansions

Two notable houses stand on the west side of the Markt. The **Bouchoute House** (Huis Bouchoute; closed to the public), on the western side at No. 15, is where England's exiled King Charles II stayed in 1656–7. Built in 1480, it was restored in 1995 to the original Gothic style. Note the octagonal compass and weathervane (1682) on the roof, which helped merchants to judge their ship's chances of entering or leaving port.

The **Craenenburg Café**, see ❶, occupies the opposite corner of Sint-Amandstraat – a pleasant pedestrianised street with several cafés. This former residence for knights and ladies in the service of the count of Flanders offered a good view from its upper windows of tournaments held on the square.

In 1488, angry townsmen incarcerated Maximilian of Austria, widower of Mary of Burgundy, in a room of the house for 100 days, after he imposed new taxes on them. His advisers were tortured in

A much-photographed view of the Dijver

rooms below. The hostage-taking of the Crown Prince of the House of Habsburg (later Holy Roman Emperor) was the final straw in a series of disputes between the people of Bruges and their rulers: Maximilian was freed after pledging to respect the townspeople's privileges, but he went back on his word, awarded the trading privileges to Antwerp and

Freedom fighters

The statue on the Markt honours two leaders of a Flemish revolt against the French, provoked by a dispute over trading rights of English wool. At dawn on 18 May 1302, butcher Jan Breydel and weaver Pieter de Coninck led an army of craftsmen from house to house, slaughtering anyone identified as French. In response, French King Philip IV raised an army of knights, who clashed with the Flemish militia two months later, on 11 July near Kortrijk. Their horses floundering in the streams and ditches that criss-crossed the field, the French noblemen fell victim to the well-organised militia; at least 1,000 knights were killed, allowing the Flemings to claim the prize that gave the conflict its name: the Battle of the Golden Spurs. Interest in the battle was renewed with the 1838 publication of the historical novel *The Lion of Flanders* by Hendrik Conscience; the statue was erected in 1887. Every year, 11 July is still marked as the official celebration of the Flemish Community.

shifted his court to Ghent. The golden age of Burgundian Bruges was over.

MILITARY CHAPEL

Follow the west flank of the Market Halls along Hallestraat, turn right into Oude Burg then immediately left under the triumphal arch into Kartuizerinnenstraat, named after a Carthusian convent that moved into the city for protection during the religious troubles of the Reformation in 1578. A surviving part of the former abbey at the bend in the street is occupied by the city's social services department. The adjoining former church of the Carthusian nuns (1716) is now a **Military Chapel** ❹ (Militaire Kapel) and war monument: its facade bears plaques commemorating people from Bruges who lost their lives in the two world wars.

DIJVER

Follow Kartuizerinnenstraat around the bend, passing the **Orangerie** hotel with its lovely terrace, (see page 96), and join Wollestraat, which leads to the **Dijver**, a canalised offshoot of the River Reie. On the left before the bridge, at No. 35, is the 15th-century Pérez de Malvenda mansion, a shop selling Belgian specialities, with a bar, **2be**, attached, see ❷.

Cross the **Sint-Jan Nepomucenusbrug** (St John of Nepomuk Bridge), with a statue (1767) of the Czech martyr,

Inside the Groeninge Museum

who was drowned in the River Vltava (or Moldau) in Prague by King Wenceslas IV in 1393 for refusing to divulge the secrets of the confessional.

Turn right after the bridge. A small **craft and antiques market** takes place by the canal at weekends and public holidays (mid-Mar–mid-Nov 10am–6pm).

GROENINGE MUSEUM

A visit to the **Groeninge Museum** ❺ (Groeningemuseum; Dijver 12; www.museabrugge.be; Tue–Sun 9.30am–5pm; charge) is a highlight of any visit to Bruges. Tucked behind a garden off the Dijver, the museum traces the development of art in the Low Countries from the 15th to the 21st century, including works by the Early Netherlandish painters, or 'Flemish Primitives', who were so active in Bruges. The collection is arranged chronologically, so visitors with little time may choose to concentrate on the first few rooms.

Flemish Primitives

Jan van Eyck (1390–1441) spent much of his career in Bruges and is seen as co-founder of the Flemish Primitives Movement, along with Brussels-based Rogier van der Weyden and the Master of Flemalle in Tournai. Credited with perfecting the technique of oil painting, van Eyck mixed powdered colours, egg white, water and resin to create a paint formula that allowed for a greater variety of colour and thinner application. The recipe remained a fiercely guarded secret among Netherlandish artists until the end of the 15th century.

Van Eyck's magnificent *Madonna and Child with Canon Joris van der Paele* (1436) is typical of the realism that characterised the style: characters, clothing and decoration are depicted in minute detail – the aged canon who sponsored the painting appears in poor health – while at the same time the painting is dripping with symbolism, such as the colour of the robes worn by the four adult characters, which echo the heraldic colours of Bruges. The same close observation of detail can be seen in the *Portrait of Margareta van Eyck* (1439), the artist's wife.

Five painters developed the movement later in the 15th century, and the Groeninge houses works by four of them: Petrus Christus, Hans Memling, Gerard David and Hugo van der Goes; St Saviour's Cathedral has an important work by the fifth, Leuven-based Dirk Bouts.

Hans Memling's altarpiece painted on commission for St James's Church in Bruges, the *Moreel Triptych* (1484) is the earliest large family portrait in the Low Countries, and appears at once realistic and otherworldly. The most memorable picture for many may be Gerard David's *Judgement of Cambyses* (1498), a study of a corrupt judge being skinned alive, which was hung in the Bruges city council chamber as a cautionary tale for lawmakers.

Arentshuis

Renaissance

The fantastical world of Hieronymus Bosch, seen here in his *Last Judgement* (early 16th century), is in a class of its own, but its themes – a reflection on the fate of sinners in the afterlife – echo the economic uncertainty and malaise of the late Middle Ages.

Jan Provoost was the most significant artist of the Renaissance in Bruges; he travelled to the Holy Land and Italy, and designed the decoration for the visit of Charles V to Bruges in 1520. But his own *Last Judgement* (1525) was censored 25 years after it was painted: a detail showing damned members of the clergy was overpainted following orders from Charles V forbidding the negative depiction of churchmen and women. The offending image was only uncovered in 1965. Lancelot Blondeel and Pieter Pourbus are two other significant Bruges artists of the period whose works are also on show.

17th and 18th centuries

Paintings of the Baroque and Rococo period started to shift away from purely religious and devotional themes to more purely diverting family portraits, landscapes and still lifes, suitable for hanging in drawing rooms rather than churches. Jacob van Oost the Elder (1601–71) marked a transition point, painting altarpieces as well as portraits for the Bruges bourgeoisie. Jan Antoon Garemijn (1712–99), meanwhile, delighted in the bustle of everyday life: his *The Pandreitje in Bruges* (1778) depicts the local street market.

19th century

Belgium greeted independence in 1830 with a renewed search for artistic and national identity. Emile Claus (1849–1924) invented Luminism, based on Impressionism, while Antwerp painter Henry van de Velde was one of the pioneers of Art Nouveau in Belgium. Mystical Symbolism struck a chord in Bruges, a 'dead town' in the process of being rediscovered. Works by Fernand Khnopff, Leon Spilliaert and William Degouve de Nuncques show the decaying beauty of the poverty-stricken city.

20th century

There is also a fine selection of 20th-century works, for example by Flemish Expressionists Gustave De Smet, Constant Permeke and Gustave van de Woestyne, who sought to express feelings and atmosphere through muted colours in scenes of everyday rural and industrial life. In wild contrast, they were followed by Belgian Surrealists Paul Delvaux and René Magritte, who used a realistic style to depict dreams and the unconscious mind.

A large and varied collection of post-1945 art, shown in rotation due to space restrictions, reflects the artistic styles that have flowered in the past 60 years, with works by conceptual artist Marcel Broodthaers, the Cobra Move-

Groenige fountain   *Gruuthuse*

ment's Pierre Alechinsky and Minimal-
ist Amédée Cortier.

ARENTSHUIS

The **Arentshuis** ❻ (www.museabrugge.
be; Tue–Sun 9.30am–5pm; charge) is
a museum housed in a mansion, set in
a garden neighbouring the Groeninge.
Downstairs is used mainly for temporary exhibitions, often devoted to art
on paper (printmaking, drawing and
photography). The upper floor contains
works by Frank Brangwyn (1867–1956),
a Welsh artist who was an apprentice to
William Morris and follower of the Arts
and Crafts Movement. Born in Bruges,
Brangwyn donated a large body of his
work to the city in 1936. As well as decorative commissions such as murals,
carpets, stained glass and furniture,
Brangwyn never forgot his years as an
impoverished artist, painting workers in
docks and factories, and those living on
the margins of society.

GRUUTHUSE

Return to the Dijver, continue west, and
turn into the courtyard of the turreted
Gothic **Palace of the Lords of Gruuthuse** ❼, the largest of the city's historical museums (www.museabrugge.be;
charge; closed for major renovations
until the end of 2014). The palace was
built in 1465 by a powerful family that
had a monopoly on the sale of *gruut*, a
herb mixture used to flavour beer (the

herbs are shown growing in the courtyard of nearby St John's Hospital).

The panelled and beamed interior
offers a peek into how the wealthy lived
during the Burgundian era, while the
private oratory upstairs that adjoins the
Church of Our Lady (see page 32)
gives you an idea of the importance of
this particular family.

The valuable and eclectic items on
display – 17th-century tapestries, devotional items and sculptures, 15th-cen-
tury waffle irons, articles belonging to
the city guilds and even a used guillo-
tine – evoke daily life in Bruges from the
15th to the 19th centuries.

Food and Drink

❶ CRAENENBURG CAFÉ

Markt 16; tel: 050 33 34 02;
www.craenenburg.be; daily 7.30am–
midnight; €€
The best-known café in Bruges is today a
traditional Flemish brasserie. It's a nice
spot for breakfast on a sunny day.

❷ 2BE

Wollestraat 53; tel: 050 61 12 22; www.2-
be.biz; daily 9.30am–7.30pm; € (drinks)
The historic property with the most
picturesque terrace in town serves drinks
during shop hours, weather permitting.
Given the shop's focus on Belgian
specialities, this is the ideal spot to sample
a local beer.

Canalside view of Old St John's Hospital

MEMLING TO THE BEGUINAGE

This route wends its way through the beguiling south of this egg-shaped city, where time appears to have stood still for centuries. Do not leave Bruges without visiting the two highlights mentioned in the title.

DISTANCE: 2.5km (1.5 miles)
TIME: A half day
START: Archaeology Museum
END: Dijver
POINTS TO NOTE: Due to the popularity of this area, try to visit early in the morning or late in the afternoon. This route could follow on from route 2, or before it if both are done in reverse.

The lush south of the city is Bruges at its most charming. Small brick houses nestle close together, their step-gables reaching tentatively up to the wide sky; secretive canals too narrow for navigation are glimpsed between houses, and nuns clad in the traditional robes of a beguine stride through carpets of daffodils on their way to prayer. Along the way are a museum with world-class paintings by Hans Memling and the only working brewery in Bruges. The narrow streets on this walk are also among the most perpetually crowded in the city, as well as the route of horse-drawn carriages, so pick your moment wisely.

ARCHAEOLOGY MUSEUM

In the former eye clinic of Old St John's Hospital, the **Archaeology Museum** ❶ (Bruggemuseum-Archeologie; Mariastraat 36a; www.museabrugge.be; Tue–Sun 9.30am–12.30pm, 1.30–5pm; charge) is an innovative, hands-on exploration of the development of Bruges from the Stone Age to the present, with interactive exhibits designed around educational panels and artefacts, and with an interior styled like a real-life dig. Good fun for children.

HOSPITAL MUSEUM – MEMLING IN ST JOHN'S

Old St John's Hospital (Oud Sint-Jan-shospitaal) is an architectural treat, one of the best-preserved medieval hospitals in Europe, where religious orders cared for pilgrims, travellers and the sick.

The large complex of buildings contains the excellent **Hospital Museum – Memling in St John's** ❷ (Hospitaalmuseum – Memling in Sint Jan; www.museabrugge.be; Tue–Sun 9.30am–

Inside the Hospital Museum

5pm; charge), where the highlight is a collection of paintings by German-born Hans Memling (c.1440–94), who lived in Bruges from 1465 until his death. Four of the six works on show were commissioned specially for the hospital chapel, where they are still displayed, by two sisters who worked here. Among them is the exquisite *Shrine of St Ursula* (c.1489), a wooden reliquary shaped like a Gothic church and painted with scenes from the life of the martyr.

Other exhibits in the museum describe the history of medical care, illustrated with some eye-popping documents, artworks and surgical instruments.

Outside, beneath the arch to the courtyard, the former hospital **pharmacy** (same days and times but closed 11.45am–2pm) can also be visited; it contains a carved relief showing patients sleeping two to a bed. The nearby **herb garden** is planted with lady's mantle, bog myrtle and bay laurel, the herbs required to make the historic beer flavouring, *gruut*. Wander around the 19th-century hospital wards (now a conference centre) and courtyard.

Overlooking the water, **B-In** is a trendy bar you might want to return to for some after-dark partying, see ❶.

WALPLEIN

Return to Mariastraat and walk south, keeping the Church of Our Lady (see page 32) on your left.

Take the second right to **Walplein**, a pretty square with cafés and touristy shops. At No. 26, the **Half Moon Brewery** ❸ (Brouwerij De

Whitewashed houses at the Beguinage

Halve Maan; www.halvemaan.be; daily 10am–6pm) is the sole surviving working brewery in Bruges, and a popular tavern and brasserie, serving varied ales and food. Records note the existence of a brewery named Die Maene (The Moon) on Walplein since 1564. This one has been run by the same family since 1856. The house brew is Brugse Zot (Bruges Fool, after the local nickname), created after they sold their well-known Straffe Hendrik (Strong Henry) to another producer. Guided tours (hourly, Sun–Fri 11am–3/4pm, Sat until 5pm; charge) of the museum and brewery include a panoramic view from the top of the building.

BEGUINAGE

Exit Walplein at its southern end – there's an attractive eatery here, **Salade Folle**, see ➋ – and turn right into Wijngaardstraat. Further down, at the green, turn right across the bridge, to enter one of the most magical spots in Bruges: the **Princely Beguinage Ten Wijngaarde** ➍ (Prinselijk Begijnhof Ten Wijngaarde; Wijngaardplein; daily 6.30am–6.30pm), founded in 1245 as a community for beguines: pious lay-women, who, without taking lifetime vows like nuns, opted for solitude and devotion, helping the poor, teaching and preaching.

Early beguines, many of them women of independent means, lived alone in society. They began living in walled communities in response to hostility voiced by (male) religious authorities. At a time when society had no place for women outside the family or the Church, the beguinage offered protection. An inscription over the Bruges beguinage gateway – Sauvegarde (safeguard) – attests to the Duchy of Burgundy's guarantee to protect the beguines and defend their independence.

Beguinage enclosure
The tranquil courtyard – best seen in spring, carpeted with flowers – is surrounded by whitewashed houses, built in the 18th century to replace the original timber structures. One of 13 surviving beguinages in Belgium, recognised jointly as a Unesco World Heritage Site, the Bruges beguinage saw its last beguine leave in 1927. Since then, it has been occupied by a community of Benedictine nuns, a retreat centre and laypeople. It takes its name – Wijngaarde – from the vineyard that used to occupy this area, where grapes were grown for making vinegar. Visitors are asked to respect the quiet atmosphere within the enclosure.

Beguine's House Museum
In a small house in the corner of the courtyard, **Beguine's House Museum** ➎ (Begijnhuisje Museum; Begijnhof 30; tel: 050 33 00 11; Mon–Sat 10am–5pm, Sun 2.30–5pm; charge) recreates the living quarters of a beguine: two simple rooms with a small

Benedictine nun

cloister garden and well. It is staffed by the Benedictine nuns who inhabit part of the Beguinage.

Beguinage Church

The **Beguinage Church** (Begijnhofkerk; tel: 050 33 00 11; daily 7am–12.15pm, 3–6pm; free) – full name Our Lady of Consolation of Spermalie (Onze-Lieve-Vrouw van Troost van Spermalie) – dates from 1245, but was rebuilt in 1605 following a fire, and given a Baroque makeover around 1700. The only object saved from the fire is a wooden (now gilded) statue of the Madonna (1300) on the side altar. Services held by the nuns are open to the public and include Gregorian sung offices.

MINNEWATER

Cross the courtyard past the church, and exit at the southern gate, which brings you to the **Minnewater**, aka the Lake of Love. Fringed with weeping willows, this pretty lake was once a major interior port, the Binnenwater, where up to 150 boats and barges could dock. It is fed from the perimeter and Ghent canals. The pink brick lock-house (Sashuis), built in 1519, regulates the level of water in the city canals.

Victor Hugo is said to have coined the 'Lac d'Amour' title when he visited in 1837. Others say the name comes from the medieval Dutch *minne*, meaning love. Another legend has it that Minna was a Saxon maiden, whose lover returned from battle to find her dead of exposure having fled her father's house rather than marry his chosen suitor. He built a dyke and created a lake over her grave.

Powder Tower

Walk to the end of the lake. The tower to the right of the bridge is the **Powder Tower ⑥** (Poertoren), a 1398 defensive tower for the former harbour, named after the gunpowder that was stocked within. Walk across the **Minnewaterbrug** (Minnewater Bridge), which gives a lovely view back over the lake.

Minnewater Park

Make your way north through the **Minnewater Park**. In summer, this lush glade is the venue for musical happenings, including, in the second week of July, the Cactus Festival, an established rock music event that draws international stars. On the left, overlooking the lake, is the Minnewater Castle (Kasteel Minnewater), a château-style former restaurant now closed following bankruptcy. At the exit of the park, make a right turn on Arsenalstraat.

DE VOS ALMSHOUSE

Take the first left, Noordstraat. At Nos 6–14, set around a beautifully tended garden, is the **De Vos Almshouse ⑦** (Godshuis De Vos), one of many such residences in Bruges, built by wealthy families from the 14th century and

Romantic Minnewater

today maintained as homes for the elderly (see feature, below). This almshouse was built in 1713 and the original eight dwellings have since been converted to six, plus a chapel.

DIAMOND MUSEUM

Rejoin Wijngaardstraat and turn right. On the right is a simple but decent café-restaurant, **De Wijngaert**, see ③.

Almshouses

The 46 almshouses *(godshuizen)* that survive in Bruges are peculiar to Flanders. They were built from the 14th century on, either by wealthy families as housing for the poor, sick or elderly, or by trade organisations for their retired members or widows. Frequently named after their benefactor, they comprised a group of tiny one-up one-down white-washed houses, plus a chapel, shared privy and garden, a patch of which was allotted to each house. The generous donation was not made for altruistic reasons alone: rich burghers saw their charitable act as an investment that would ensure their place in heaven. Indeed, the chapels built within each complex were explicitly intended for residents to pray for the souls of their benefactors. Most of the almshouses are now owned and run by the city social services department. Visitors are free to enter the premises, but asked to respect the silence.

At the top is Katelijnestraat; across the street at no. 43 is the **Diamond Museum** ❽ (Diamantmuseum; www. diamondmuseum.be; daily 10.30am–5.30pm, closed mid-Jan; charge), where you can discover the little-known local origins of diamond polishing. The technique is thought to have been invented in Bruges by 15th-century goldsmith Lodewijk van Berquem. His workshop is recreated inside, along with tools of the trade, models, paintings and rock samples; there are also daily demonstrations (12.15pm and 3.15pm) of the technique. This private museum is run by a family in the diamond trade, whose stores are at 5 Cordoeaniersstraat and 43 Katelijnestraat.

MORE ALMSHOUSES

Walking north towards Mariastraat, if it's time for lunch or dinner there's the excellent **Indian Tandoori** restaurant nearby, see ❹. Then turn right into Nieuwe Gentweg to visit more adorable almshouses: the **St Joseph and De Meulenaere Almshouses** ❾ (Godshuizen Sint-Jozef en De Meulenaere) at Nos 8–22. Built in 1613, they are two of the loveliest almshouses in the city, and also accessible, since their garden is usually open. Built around a shared courtyard garden with cottage-style mixed borders, there is also a tiny chapel and a water pump.

Exit the gate and cross the road. Turn directly into Groeninge, an unexpectedly

Powder Tower

De Meulenaere Almshouse

bucolic lane that wends its path around the garden of the Groeninge Museum (see page 43) – passing a top-notch restaurant on the way, **Den Gouden Harynck**, see ❺ – and back to the Dijver, where this walk ends.

Food and Drink

❶ B-IN

Zonnekemeers – Oud Sint-Jan; tel: 050 31 13 00; www.b-in.be; Tue–Sat 11am–2am, restaurant: noon–2.30pm, 6.30–10pm; €€

Club Brugge players and other local celebs like to mingle at this hip lounge bar with a lovely terrace in the pedestrianised courtyard behind St John's Hospital. It's also a restaurant, but one where style takes precedence over substance, so dress to impress. There are often live DJs on Friday and Saturday.

❷ SALADE FOLLE

Walplein 13–14; tel: 050 34 94 43; www.saladefolle.com; Tue–Sat noon–6pm; €

In a bright, contemporary interior behind an old brick facade, this informal establishment serves a lighter menu than your average Belgian restaurant – soup, salad, quiche or pasta, including several vegetarian options – as well as dessert and ices.

❸ DE WIJNGAERT

Wijngaardstraat 15; tel: 050 33 69 18; www.wijngaert.com; Thur–Tue noon–3pm, 6–10pm, café service from 11am, winter closed Wed–Thur; €

This grill restaurant, bar and tearoom along the well-worn tourist groove between the Beguinage and Onze-Lieve-Vrouwekerk is a reasonable, no-frills option for well-prepared mussels, ribs or more. The house sangria is a speciality.

❹ INDIAN TANDOORI

Oude Gentweg 11; tel: 050 34 58 26; www.indiantandoori.be; Wed–Mon noon–2.30pm, 6–11pm; €

Although this spot is right in the heart of tourist town, it is just off the main drag and so often overlooked. Seek it out for subtly spiced, authentic dishes from the Subcontinent, made with the freshest ingredients and served with understated grace. The best Indian food in town.

❺ DEN GOUDEN HARYNCK

Groeninge 25; tel: 050 33 76 37; www.goudenharynck.be; Tue–Fri noon–2pm, 7–9pm, Sat 7–9pm, closed three weeks from mid-July–early Aug; €€€€

Taking its name from the 17th-century former fishmonger's shop that it occupies, this luxurious restaurant is the showcase for chef Philippe Serruys. A master of French gastronomy, Serruys draws on Bruges's trading past to mingle local and exotic flavours to fantastic effect.

Jerusalem Church

SINT-ANNA

The quiet district of Sint-Anna is famed for its small-scale and offbeat attractions: a crusader's mausoleum, ancient crossbowmen's club, lace centre, windmills and museums of folklore and poetry. At a relaxed pace, you could spend the best part of a day ambling around here.

DISTANCE: 2.5km (1.5 miles)
TIME: 3 hours
START: St Anne's Church
END: Café Vlissinghe
POINTS TO NOTE: This route could follow on from the end of No. 3, by crossing the Sint-Annabrug to reach the start. It is a good walk for children, as the Folklore Museum has much to keep them entertained, and for all but tiny ones the windmill is fun. Tue–Sat is the ideal time to do it; avoid Sun, when the Jerusalem Church, a highlight, is closed.

Away from the centre, the Sint-Anna district has few shops or cafés, and is characterised by rows of simple terraced houses and a bucolic air. Ideal for a stroll, it offers an insight into the history of everyday life in Bruges. Peek inside a former almshouse, discover the gruelling lot of a lace-maker and peep over high walls into the crossbowmen's club. Then relax on a grassy canal bank with a beer.

SINT-ANNA

Start on Sint-Annaplein at **St Anne's Church ❶** (Sint-Annakerk; Apr–Sept Mon–Sat 10am–noon and 2–5pm, Sun 2–5pm), a 1624 Baroque edifice, with ornate carving inside. The counter on the left as you enter used to be where the poor of the parish would mark registers each time they attended mass, so they could receive tokens for food and clothing on feast days. Leave the square at the eastern end, and then turn right into Jeruzalemstraat.

Jerusalem Church

The striking **Jerusalem Church ❷** (Jeruzalemkerk; Peperstraat; www.kant centrum.com; Mon–Sat 10am–5pm; charge; includes entry to Lace Centre) was built in 1428–65 by a family of Genoan merchants based in Bruges. Pieter Adornes returned from a pilgrimage to the Holy Land to build this copy of the Church of the Holy Sepulchre and his son Anselm completed it. A mixture of Byzantine and Gothic styles, it has been spared destruction thanks to its

Traditional lace-making   *Altar in the Jerusalem Church*

private chapel status and is remarkably well preserved, boasting 16th-century stained glass.

Anselm was murdered in Scotland in 1483 while on a diplomatic mission and was buried in Linlithgow, but his heart was brought back to Bruges to be laid to rest with his wife, Margaretha. Their marble sarcophagus dominates the interior; later generations of the family are buried beneath the church and recalled in coats of arms on the walls. An altar carved with skulls and bones and a copy of Christ's memorial tomb in the crypt complete the deathly ambience.

Lace Centre

On the same entrance ticket as the Jerusalem Church, the **Lace Centre** (Kantcentrum; details and times as Jerusalem Church) is a non-profit foundation that organises lace-making courses and holds demonstrations of the craft of bobbin lace every afternoon. Examples of lace-work are displayed off the courtyard in six tiny almshouses that the Adornes family built for the poor in the 15th century. Around the corner, at No. 11 Balstraat is a shop, **'t Apostelientje** (www.apostelientje.be; Mon and Wed– Sat 9.30am–12.15pm, 1.15–5pm, Sun 10am–1pm), selling local lace and craft supplies.

Museum of Folklore

Walk north up Balstraat. Near the end, at No. 43, is the **Museum of Folklore** ❸ (Bruggemuseum – Volk- skunde; www.museabrugge.be; Tue– Sun 9.30am–5pm; charge), in a row of 17th-century whitewashed cottages that were once the almshouse of the Shoemakers' Guild. Each room recon- structs a 19th-century interior: a pri- mary-school class, clogmaker's and milliner's workshops, a pharmacist and a confectioner (with sweet-mak- ing demonstrations) among others. In summer, visitors can play with tra- ditional toys and games in the gar- den; and the visit ends, charmingly, in an old ale house, **The Black Cat** (De Zwarte Kat).

Lace-making

By the mid-1800s, Bruges was the poorest city in Belgium, dependent on home-based textile manufacture and unable to compete with industrialised cities. In the 1840s, the lace-making industry provided steady employment – and starvation wages – for 10,000 women and girls (nearly a quarter of the population). They worked 12 hours a day yet still needed to resort to prosti- tution to pay for food. Today, most lace sold is machine-made and imported, although some is still handmade locally. The most popular kind of lace made in Bruges is bobbin lace, created using a technique where threads of silk, linen or cotton on as many as 700 bobbins are crossed and braided around a frame- work of pins.

Windmill in the Ring Canal Park

English Convent

At the top of Balstraat, cross Rolweg and continue straight up Speelmansstraat, turning right on Carmersstraat. On the left at No. 85 is the **English Convent** (Engels Klooster; www.the-english-convent.be; Mon–Sat 2–3.30pm, 4.15–5.30pm), established in the wake of England's Dissolution of the Monasteries under King Henry VIII. The convent and its church were a hub for the city's former English colony, which in the 1860s numbered 1,200. It is now a guesthouse for groups and individuals on retreat.

St Sebastian Archers' Guild

Further up Carmersstraat at No. 174 is the skinny hexagonal tower of the **St Sebastian Archers' Guild ❹** (Schuttersgilde Sint-Sebastiaan; www.sebastiaans

gilde.be; May–Sept Tue–Thur 10am–noon, Sat 2–5pm, Oct–Apr Tue–Thur and Sat 2–5pm; charge). This ancient longbow club dates from the time of the Crusades; past members include England's King Charles II, who paid for the banqueting hall while in exile in Bruges from Oliver Cromwell. Charles formed a royal regiment of guards here, which accompanied him to London when the monarchy was restored in 1660. All British monarchs since have been honorary members of the guild, whose collection contains arms, furnishings, gold and silver plate, and other artworks.

ST JOHN'S HOUSE MILL

The green space ahead is dominated by the **St John's House Mill ❺** (Sint-

Apse detail, English Convent

Kruispoort

Janshuismolen; Kruisvest; www.musea brugge.be; May–Aug Tue–Sun 9.30am–12.30pm, 1.30–5pm, Sept Sat–Sun 9.30am–12.30pm, 1.30–5pm; charge), one of four timber-stilt windmills that dot the canalside park along the northeastern city perimeter, left here as a reminder of the 29 that once dotted the ramparts, mainly milling grain. In summer, this particular mill, which earned its living from 1770–1914, is cranked back into action and open to the public. Access is via a vertiginous staircase.

HOLY CROSS GATE

Walk south through the park past the next mill, Bonne Chieremolen (closed to the public), to the **Kruispoort** ❻ (Holy Cross Gate), one of the entries to the city from the second town wall of 1297. This structure dates from the early 15th century, but has been much rebuilt. Seen from outside, the gate has two fortified towers, joined by a battlement through which stones or molten lead could be dropped on invaders. In contrast, from within the walls residents saw an elegant portal, with octagonal turrets and dripstone moulding.

GUIDO GEZELLE MUSEUM

Retrace your steps north. On the left is another old archery club set in a garden, visible by its tall target mast. Unlike at St Sebastian's, the chaps of **St George's**

Archers' Guild (Schuttersgilde Sint-Joris; Stijn Streuvelsstraat 59; tel: 050 33 54 08; open by prior arrangement only) are crossbowmen.

Continue up Kruisvest and turn left on Rolweg. At No. 64, the **Guido Gezelle Museum** ❼ (www.museabrugge.be; Tue–Sun 9.30am–12.30pm, 1.30–5pm; charge) is the childhood home of the poet-priest (1830–99). Gezelle fought to establish Flemish as a literary language distinct from Netherlandish Dutch. His life and work are recalled in the house, and the large walled garden is charming.

Café Vlissinghe

Follow Rolweg to the end, turn right onto Jeruzalemstraat, and second left on Blekersstraat. The oldest café in Bruges, **Vlissinghe**, see ❶, can be found down this narrow street, a fitting place to end this walk.

Rosary Quay

FISH MARKET TO ASTRID PARK

This route takes in a succession of scenic quaysides, along canals punctuated with lichen-covered bridges. It then follows a waterway through a laid-back former industrial quarter to end in a park much loved by locals.

DISTANCE: 2km (1.25 miles)
TIME: 1.5 hours
START: Fish Market
END: Astrid Park
POINTS TO NOTE: This outdoor route is best for a dry day. It is good for children, as it ends in a park with a playground.

Dutch rule

After Napoleon's defeat at Waterloo in 1815, the Congress of Vienna united the Northern and Southern Netherlands under the Protestant rule of William I of Orange to create a buffer against France. This union, after 200 years of separation, was unpopular in Catholic Bruges, among all but a small Protestant minority. Within 15 years, the Southerners organised a rebellion in Brussels, which Dutch forces barely attempted to suppress. When it declared independence in 1830, the Southern Netherlands became Belgium, a self-governing region for the first time.

It is a sign of how compact Bruges is that on this relatively short route you can wander from the most photographed view in the city to an ignored stretch of canal where the houseboats and grassy banks make it feel like a country village.

FISH MARKET

The neoclassical, colonnaded **Fish Market ❶** (Vismarkt), built 1820−1, is one of few notable structures dating from the period of Dutch rule. From Tuesday to Saturday mornings, fishmongers lay out the morning's catch fresh from nearby coastal ports Zeebrugge and Ostend. Right alongside, restaurant **De Visscherie** (see page 106), is the go-to address for fish and seafood specialities. Craft stalls occupy a number of the stands at other times.

ROSARY QUAY

Leave the Fish Market by the south, turning right on Braambergstraat. This takes you past two eating and drinking options for now or later, **Wijnbar Est**,

Fish Market coat of arms   *Groenerei*

see ❶, and **De Gastro**, see ❷, to one of the most picturesque spots in Bruges: the view over the canal basin from **Rozenhoedkaai** ❷ (Rosary Quay).

Winston Churchill is one of many artists, amateur and professional, to have painted the scene from this spot, picking out the warm patina of medieval brickwork reflected in the canal, capped by the view to the Belfry beyond. The maudlin protagonist in Georges Rodenbach's novel *Bruges-la-Morte* occupied a house on this quayside, which in turn inspired the 1906 poem *Quai du Rosaire* by Rainer Maria Rilke.

TANNERS' SQUARE

Retrace your steps a little and turn left into **Huidenvettersplein** ❸ (Tanners' Square). Between Easter and October, the small square is packed with restau-

Tranquil Coupure

rant tables and street painters. The former Tanners' Guildhouse (1630–1) on the west side of the square is now an posh restaurant, 't Huidevettershuis. Cross the square and exit at the northeastern corner. On the left, the house by the jetty is the former **Fishmongers' Corporation House**; note the fishy coat of arms above the door.

GROENEREI

This is one achingly pretty stretch of canal. Keep the canal to your left, passing the Fish Market on the right. The view across the water shows the rear of the Town Hall and the surviving 16th-century facade of the Liberty of Bruges Palace, which from the Burg side is hidden by an 18th-century addition. Continue along Steenhouwersdijk, which turns into tree-lined **Groenerei**. Pass **Meebrug** and **Peerdenbrug**, two stone bridges that create lovely reflections beneath their arches. Stand on Peerdenbrug to admire the view back to the tower of St Saviour's Cathedral. On the right, at Nos 8–12, the **Pelican Almshouse** ❹ (Godshuis De Pelikaan) can be identified by the relief of a pelican (a symbol of Christ) feeding its young. Built in 1634, it was an almshouse and hospital for the poor.

ALONG THE COUPURE

Follow the narrow canalside path as it bends right, passing the lovely Het Hemelhuis sauna at No. 16. The tourist boats peel off left to the north, while we head south towards a more tranquil quarter of the city. Cross Predikherenstraat and continue straight over alongside the water. This wider portion of canal, the **Coupure**, reflects its industrial heritage. It was dug in 1752 to allow river traffic from Ghent a shorter route via Sint-Annarei to the Langerei, bypassing the winding waterways through the centre. It retained an industrial character until the start of World War II. The southern end is a popular mooring spot for houseboats and cabin cruisers, and for fishermen trying their luck from the quay.

Bistro option
Turn left to cross the **Coupurebrug** (Coupure Bridge) and then right to follow the canal's eastern bank south. If it's time for a meal, make the most of a good spot on the corner by the bridge, **Bistro de Schaar**, see ❸.

Conzett Bridge
On the grassy square a little further south is a small statue of a girl, *Marieke*, inspired by the character in Jacques Brel's song *Ai Marieke*. At the end, turn right to cross back across the water via the modern **Conzettbrug** ❺ (Conzett Bridge), a cycle- and footbridge designed by Swiss engineer Jürg Conzett to mark Bruges's year as European Capital of Culture in 2002.

Astrid Park fountain

Scrolls of rusting metal span the walkway of weather-washed timber, forming a handy link in the park.

GHENT GATE

Continue along the footpath leading southwest from Conzettbrug to the **Ghent Gate ❻** (Gentpoort; Thur–Sun 9.30am–12.30pm, 1.30-5pm; charge), one of four surviving medieval city gates that served a dual role as fortification as well as to monitor imports and exports in and out. An exhibition inside tells the history of the city's gates.

ASTRID PARK

Turn back towards the city centre up Gentpoortstraat, a local shopping street, to the southern tip of **Astrid Park ❼** (Astridpark). Named after Queen Astrid (1905–35), the Swedish-born consort of King Leopold III who died tragically young in a motor accident, it is one of the largest parks in the city, with a pond, kids' playground and a colourful bandstand. The park is still known among locals as the 'Botanieken Hof', recalling its origins as a botanical garden when it was created in 1850 on the site of a former Franciscan friary. The **St Magdalene's Church** (Heilige Magdalenakerk) (1851–3) sits on the southern corner of the park.

A pleasant café, **L'Estaminet**, faces the northern edge of the park at the end of this walk, see ❹.

Food and Drink

❶ WIJNBAR EST
Braambergstraat 7; tel: 050 33 38 39; www.wijnbarest.be; Thur–Mon 4pm–midnight; €€
This popular wine bar, which has a long drinks menu, serves light and main meals and puts on live music on Sunday evenings.

❷ DE GASTRO
Braambergstraat 6; tel: 050 34 15 24; www.degastro.be; daily 11am–3pm, 6–10pm, closed Thur Sept–June; €
This stylish address has a great-value menu, from snacks to Belgian classics and fusion-inspired dishes. Does pancakes and waffles in the afternoon.

❸ BISTRO DE SCHAAR
Hooistraat 2; tel: 050 33 59 79; www.bistrodeschaar.be; Fri–Tue noon–2.30pm, 6–10pm; €€
This popular neighbourhood bistro has an open grill-fire and specialises in grilled fish and meat. Best to reserve.

❹ L'ESTAMINET
Park 5; tel: 050 33 09 16; daily 11am–late; €
Open since 1900, this family-friendly café gets packed on a Sunday afternoon, after the obligatory park stroll. It serves simple bar meals, plays the blues and sometimes hosts live music.

City Theatre's opulent interior

MERCHANTS' QUARTER

The hub of international trade in the 14th century has numerous landmarks that evoke the city's commercial heyday. This route is not only a journey back in time; it is a reminder that markets that rise must also fall.

DISTANCE: 1.5km (1 mile)
TIME: 2.5 hours
START/END: City Theatre
POINTS TO NOTE: This route starts and ends near the Markt, just up Vlamingstraat to the north. It has few indoor sights on its route, so take an umbrella if the weather looks dodgy.

By the 14th century, Bruges's cloth-making industry was in decline. Commerce became its fortune: as a member of the Hanseatic League, it drew merchants from Castile, the Rhine, Genoa and London, along with Italian bankers, who controlled the flow of finance. This route visits the district where they lived, met and exchanged goods: sheepskin, lead and tin from England and Scotland, wine, spices and luxury products from Italy, and citrus fruits, leather and sugar from Spain. Much of the city's artistic and built heritage dates from this period: trade brought revenue through taxes, and locals grew wealthy providing services to cosmopolitan visitors.

CITY THEATRE

Our starting point is the **City Theatre** ❶ (Stadsschouwburg), built in 1867 in neo-Renaissance style by Brussels architect Gustave Saintenoy. Until the Concert Hall was built in 2002, this was the prime arts venue in town; today, it is the hub of an arts network, showing classical theatre, world music, contemporary dance and more.

Across from the theatre is the **Patisserie Servaas van Mullem**, see ❶.

MERCHANTS' HOUSES

The square at the junction of Academiestraat and Vlamingstraat was a meeting place for merchants and traders from the 13th–16th centuries. The **Genoan Lodge** ❷ (Genuese loge) at No. 33 dates from 1399; the city's coat of arms is still visible above a small side door. The bell-shaped gable was added in 1720 when the building passed to a federation of serge traders from Hondschoote near Dunkirk – hence its name, **White Serge Hall** (De Witte Saaihalle).

Detail from Ter Beurze House　　　　　*City Theatre exterior*

Fries Museum

The building is now occupied by the **Fries Museum** (Friet Museum; www.friet museum.be; daily 10am–5pm except two weeks mid-Jan; charge), devoted to the history of potatoes and chips. An important part of this history entails restoring to Belgium ownership of a food known widely as 'French fries', allegedly the result of confusion on the part of American soldiers after World War I.

Ter Beurze House

Medieval merchants who could not get bed space in their own consulate were housed by locals such as the Van der Beurze family, whose 1453 **Ter Beurze House** (Huis Ter Beurze) stands at No. 35. Such families became middlemen, introducing buyer and seller, and acting as lenders, guarantors and exchange agents until the deal was cut under their roof. This house became synony-mous with the practice, giving its name to places across Continental Europe where merchants met to fix prices for the exchange of goods: *beurs* (in Dutch) and its equivalents in other languages: *bourse*, *börse* and *bursa*. Now home to a local radio station, this was the world's first stock exchange.

Venetian and Florentine Houses

Neither the Venetian consulate at No. 37 nor the Florentine lodge at Acade-miestraat 1 has survived, but their mem-ory lives on in an **engraving** from canto 15 of Dante's *Inferno* on the side wall of the latter address (now a restaurant, **De Florentijnen**, see page 110), describ-ing Bruges's perpetual battle with the sea: 'Even as the Flemings, 'twixt Cad-sand and Bruges,/ Fearing the flood that tow'rds them hurls itself,/ Their bul-warks build to put the sea to flight.'

JAN VAN EYCKPLEIN

Turn right into Acade-miestraat, passing **Bras-serie Forestière** (see page 110), a good dining option, to **Jan van Eyck-plein ❸**, named after the 15th-century painter who made his name in Bruges. Stand by his statue for a view over these sights.

On the western side of the square is the tower of the 15th-century **Burgh-**

Spiegelrei with Jan van Eyckplein to the left

ers' **Lodge** (Poortersloge), a meeting place for bankers and merchants. From elite club, the building became a fine arts academy until 1890; today, it houses the city archives. Among visitors to the Burghers' Lodge were members of the illustrious White Bear (Witte Beer) Club, whose emblem can be seen in a niche on the corner of the building. According to legend, the white bear was the first inhabitant of Bruges and caused terror in the region until Baldwin Iron Arm, first count of Flanders, nailed it to a tree in the 9th century. It figures, with the lion, on the city's coat of arms.

Old Customs House

Across Academiestraat from the Burgher's Lodge is the pointed gable of the **Old Customs House** (Oud Tolhuis), where ships had to pay taxes on goods brought in from the outer ports of Damme and Sluis. Behind its facade is a 13th-century merchant's house, with spacious rooms on lower floors for storing goods, and living quarters upstairs. The tiny house next door was the 15th-century HQ for porters *(pijnders)*. Their back-breaking trade is evoked in stone carvings at the base of a pillar. Next door was the public weighing house. The combined buildings are now the seat of the provincial library, which holds 600 religious manuscripts and early printed books.

Spiegelrei and Spinolarei

Turn around to face the canal. Bruges has many former harbours and this –

along **Spiegelrei** and **Spinolarei** – was one of the busiest: the canal once continued to the Markt. Porters would have unloaded Castilian oranges and lemons, oriental spices, Mediterranean velvet, and Baltic fur and amber. This was the diplomatic centre of Hanseatic Bruges, with foreign consulates situated along Spiegelrei. Many of the houses retain vast vaulted storage cellars.

De Rode Steen House

At No. 8 on the square, on the corner of Spiegelrei, is **De Rode Steen**, which partly dates from the 13th century. This was the first building in Bruges awarded renovation funding, in 1877, marking the start of investment to restore the city's heritage. On the right of the steps to the door is a plaque honouring the writer Georges Rodenbach (see page 57), whose grandfather lived nearby. Keep this house on your right and head northeast up Genthof. Note the rare surviving 16th-century timber facade at No. 7.

SPANISH QUAY

Walking northeast, cross Woensdagmarkt, named after a former Wednesday vegetable market. A **statue of Hans Memling** (1871) by Hendrik Pickery now has pride of place. Then cross Oosterlingenplein (Easterners' Square) and turn left alongside the canal into the **Spaanse Loskaai** (Spanish Quay), where Spanish ships used to dock, unloading bundles of Castilian wool.

Augustinians' Bridge

Augustinians' Bridge

Triple-arched **Augustijnenbrug** ❹ (Augustinians' Bridge) was the first stone bridge in Bruges, built in 1294 by monks from a friary then situated by the canal. Legend has it there was once a tunnel under the canal by which monks would reach a convent on the other bank, for illicit trysts with nuns.

Phantom House

The House of Lamentations (Den Noodt Gods Huis) 5 on the west corner of Spanjaardstraat beside the bridge was built in 1616 by Spanish merchant Francisco de Peralta. Since the 19th century, it has been known as the **Phantom House** (Spookhuis), inspired by stories of a monk who killed the object of his devotion in a fit of passion. Their two spirits allegedly haunt the building, which has changed hands repeatedly, and been abandoned on more than one occasion.

Cross Augustinians' Bridge for a walk along some attractive canalside streets. Turn left on Augustijnenrei, cross Sint-Jorisstraat and continue straight on Pottenmakersstraat. Turn left at the end, crossing back over Ezelbrug to the south side of the canal, and turn left into Grauwwerkersstraat, which follows the canal and then bends to the right. Remember this street if you fancy some tapas at **Vino Vino**, see ❷.

BLADELIN COURT

Around the bend, turn right into Naardenstraat. The **Bladelin Court** ❺ (Hof Bladelin) at No. 19 was built around 1440 by Pieter Bladelin, treasurer to Duke Philip the Good and his Order of the Golden Fleece. The Medici Bank of Florence took over the property in 1466, and gave it an Italianate makeover. This can be seen in the **inner courtyard garden**, the only part of the building open to the public (Mon–Fri 9am–noon, 2–5pm). Stone medallions on the facade depict Lorenzo de' Medici and his wife, Clarice Orsini. It is now a retirement home.

Retrace your steps and turn right into Kuipperstraat. This leads to the rear of the theatre, where this walk began.

Food and Drink

❶ PATISSERIE SERVAAS VAN MULLEM

Vlamingstraat 56; tel: 050 33 05 15; Wed–Sun 7.30am–6pm; €
Well-dressed professionals and academics take their morning coffee over a paper at this upmarket patisserie with a small terrace.

❷ VINO VINO

Grauwwerkersstraat 15; tel: 0486 39 80 66; Tue–Sat 6pm–late; €
Sangria, Spanish tapas, blues on the sound system and a friendly owner have earned this backstreet wine bar a faithful following. Good for a romantic tête-à-tête, it is also one of the few nightlife options in town.

Crossing the Carmersbrug

LANGEREI AND ST GILES

Follow Langerei, a canal that used to be the city's trading lifeline, passing old bridges and an abbey to an ancient hospital museum and church, and returning via a sleepy quarter once favoured by stars of the early Flemish art scene.

DISTANCE: 2.5km (1.5 miles)
TIME: 2.5 hours
START: Carmersbrug
END: Café Terrastje
POINTS TO NOTE: Mainly outdoor and quite long, this route is best done on a fine day. It could be combined with an excursion to Damme, by boat, cycle or on foot (route 12), or followed by route 6 in Sint-Anna conducted in reverse, or linked with the shorter route 8 in the Merchants' Quarter.

Furs, amber, flax and honey were among the imports to medieval Bruges from its partners in the Hanseatic League, an alliance of trading cities and guilds that operated from the 13th to the 17th century. As silting progressively restricted direct access to the sea, ships would dock in the outer port of Damme, some 7km (4.5 miles) away, and then Sluis, when the route to Damme became impractical. From there, small barges would convey goods into the city along Langerei.

POTTERIEREI

Set off from the **Carmersbrug ❶** (Carmelite Bridge). Note, on its southeastern side, the carved stone monk who measures the water depth with his staff. Turn left and follow Potterierei north.

Imported goods including coal, wheat and wood were unloaded along the Langerei canal right up until World War II. The tranquil **Potterierei**, which snakes north up its eastern quayside, is still lined with historic properties; it looks its best in the afternoon sun, when dappled light filters through the plane trees that line the quay.

Episcopal Seminary

Pass the next bridge, Snaggaardbrug, and, further up, the wooden drawbridge, **Duinenbrug**. The latter takes its name from the former Cistercian **Abbey of the Dunes ❷** (Ter Duinen Abdij) at No. 72. The abbey moved to Bruges in 1627 from its previous location in Koksijde; it was threatened by encroaching seas. Following the

Our Lady of the Pottery

French Revolution, when the abbey became public property, the buildings were used successively as a military hospital, military depot and a school. In 1833, it was returned to the Church and has become the **Episcopal Seminary** (Groot-Seminarie), a college for Catholic priests.

Our Lady of the Pottery

Further up at No. 79 is the 14th-century **Our Lady of the Pottery** ❸ (Onze-Lieve-Vrouw-ter-Potterie; Tue–Sun 9.30am–12.30pm, 1.30–5pm). Once the chapel of the Potters' Guild, the church was part of a hospice founded 1276 by Augustinian nuns. Much of the complex is still a retirement home, although today's residents occupy modern buildings.

The unusual church has a double nave; the older, to the north, dates from 1359. The embroidered hangings (*c.*1565) in the side altars contain gold and silver thread, while the south nave holds possibly the oldest Netherlandish miracle statue, *Our Lady of Mons-en-Pévèle*, crafted in wood in the early 14th century and named after the 1305 battle from which it takes its name. The 16th-century tapestries flanking the left side of this nave depict miracles associated with the Virgin Mary.

The **Pottery Museum** (tel: 050 44 87 11; Tue–Sun 9.30am–12.30pm, 1.30–5pm; www.museabrugge.be; charge), in the church's former wards and cloisters, displays medical artefacts that recall the former hospice, plus furniture, Delft-

St Giles Church

ware, tapestries and a glittering array of church plate and rare manuscripts.

DAMPOORT

Continue to the end of Potterierei and **Dampoort** ❹, the former gate on the road to Damme. Pleasure cruisers and industrial barges wait here for the road-bridge to be raised over the ring canal. After the waterway to the Zwin inlet silted up, a new canal to Ostend was opened in 1622. Many large vessels today take the more recent **Boudewijnkanaal** (1896–1905) to Zeebrugge.

Cool Meadow Mill
The **Cool Meadow Mill** ❺ (Koeleweimolen; July–Aug Tue–Sun 9.30am–12.30pm, 1.30–5pm; charge; www.museabrugge.be; charge) stands beside the canal on Kruisvest, south of the bridge. Built in 1765, it is part of the city museum network and an operating grain mill open to the public in summer.

LANGEREI

Return to Dampoort and cross to the western bank of the Langerei canal via Sasplein, south of the busy road junction. At No. 2 is a handy refreshment stop, the **Bistro du Phare**, see ❶. Wander back south along Langerei, admiring the bourgeois mansions that line the canal. There is little to detain you here, although if you fancy a break, step off the street at No. 76, where an alley leads to a small garden with picnic tables behind the houses.

St Giles
After passing the Snaggaardbrug on the left, take the next right, Sint-Gilliskoorstraat. This is St Giles district, for centuries home to workers and artists, including Jan van Eyck, Hans Memling and Gerard David. Later, along with the St George's (Sint-Joris) district to the west, it was something of an English colony. Art historian James Weale (1832–1917), who is credited with discovering the works of Memling and other Flemish Primitives, lived at the junction of Sint-Jorisstraat and Clarastraat. Still a largely residential district, it retains an air of quiet detachment from the rest of the city.

Although the terraced houses in St Giles are very small, many have had windows bricked up. This practice dates back to 1800, when a window tax was levied.

St Giles Church
Entered via its western door on Baliestraat, **St Giles Church** ❻ (Sint-Gilliskerkhof; Mon–Sat 10am–noon, 2–5pm, Sun 11–5pm) was founded in 1241. Major alterations in the 15th century left it with three aisles in place of its earlier cruciform; only the chunky stone pillars inside date from the original construction. The painter Hans Memling was buried here in 1494 in the long-gone churchyard, and is remem-

bered by a plaque located beside the entrance.

Among the treasures inside are a superb organ, a polyptych (1564) by Pieter Pourbus and a cycle of paintings from 1774 by Bruges artist Jan Garemijn, depicting the history of the Trinitarian Brothers and their retrieval of white slaves from Algeria.

If you are thinking about food at this stage, try 't Oud Handbogenhof, see ②, or, a little further away, Tom's Diner (see page 111).

GOUDEN-HANDREI

From the southern side of the church take Sint-Gilliskerkstraat. At the end, turn right along Gouden-Handstraat. An English seminary used to be situated on this street. Turn left onto Torenbrug. The property on the left beside the bridge (now part of the College of Europe) was where painter Jan van Eyck lived and worked, entertaining wealthy patrons in his studio.

Over the bridge, turn left to follow the quayside of **Gouden-Handrei** back to the start of the walk. This stretch of canal is enchantingly still, reflecting the gardens and summer houses on the historic properties on the opposite bank. The light is at its best in late afternoon.

At the end of the street, turn right towards the Carmersbrug, where this walk began. It ends at the next junction, with Genthof, where there is a pleasant café, **Terrastje**, see ③.

Food and Drink

① BISTRO DU PHARE

Sasplein 2; tel: 050 34 35 90; www.duphare.be; bar Wed–Mon 11.30am–midnight; food 12.30–3pm, 6pm–midnight; €€

This music bar-brasserie has a friendly atmosphere, varied menu (Creole, Thai, steaks) and live blues and jazz bands. Busiest at night, but a pleasant spot for lunch or drinks. A large south-facing terrace beside the canal is a draw.

② 'T OUD HANDBOGENHOF

Baliestraat 6; tel: 050 33 71 18; Tue–Sat 6–9.30pm, Sun noon–1.30pm, 6–9.30pm; €€

Push the heavy door to this ancient hostelry and enter a Brueghelian scene: a beamed dining room with huge fireplace, flagstone floor and hearty Belgian cuisine. The garden to the rear is shady in fine weather.

③ TERRASTJE

Genthof 45; tel: 050 33 09 19; Sun–Tue 11am–11.30pm, Wed 11am–7pm, Fri–Sat 11am–midnight; €€

This tiny café with a large terrace, run by an English-Dutch couple, is prized for its varied menu: soup, snails, *waterzooï*, omelette and salads, plus deli platters and desserts (ices and pancakes).

Neo–Gothic Princes' Court

PRINCES' COURT AND DONKEY GATE

The dukes of Burgundy called this district home at the height of their rule in the 15th century. This route takes in the site of their former palace, a quiet park and a church adorned with treasures donated by noblemen and merchants.

DISTANCE: 3km (2 miles), or short version 1.75km (1 mile)

TIME: 1–2 hours

START/END: Eiermarkt

POINTS TO NOTE: The shorter version of this route excludes a few non-essential sights, including the Donkey Gate. Visitors should also note that St James's Church, one of the highlights of this walk, is not open from October to March.

The period of Burgundian rule in Bruges from 1384–1482 was a time of both prosperity and tension, marked by the Hundred Years War between England and France and by power struggles between the aristocracy and the trade guilds. While its rulers were at war with England, business depended on imports of English wool for cloth production. International traders in the city tired of the incessant quarrelling and, by 1457, the Hanseatic League had shifted its headquarters to Antwerp, depriving the city of income from banking and

inn-keeping. In place of cloth, the city started producing luxury items such as illuminated manuscripts, miniatures, panel paintings and cut diamonds. Bruges remained fabulously rich, thanks in part to the Burgundian court's support of the arts, but the source of its wealth – trade – had started to ebb away.

MUNTPLEIN

From **Eiermarkt** (Egg Market), with its 1761 pump adorned with the lion of Flanders and the Bruges bear from the city's coat of arms, take Geldmunt-straat to Geerwijnstraat, first right, which leads to **Muntplein ❶**. Named after the count's former coin mint *(munt)*, this small square contains an equestrian statue – *Flandria Nostra* – depicting Mary of Burgundy, who was crushed to death aged 25 (1482) by her horse when out hunting. Her death signalled an end to Burgundian rule in Bruges: Mary's husband, Maximilian I of Austria, a Habsburg, was an unpopular ruler who decamped with his court to Antwerp.

PRINCES' COURT

From Muntplein, rejoin Geldmuntstraat (*geld* means money) via the arched former gate, turn right, then right again at the next street, into Prinsenhof. The **Prinsenhof ②** (Princes' Court; see page 100), now an upscale hotel, is a neo-Gothic copy (1888) of the palace of the dukes of Burgundy, built in 1396 on this site. In its original form, the palace was seven times the size of what you can see, and stretched from Noordzandstraat to Moerstraat, surrounded by walls and battlements.

Court history

Philip the Good married Isabella of Portugal here in 1430 and founded the Order of the Golden Fleece to mark the event. The wedding banquet was held in a hall decorated with tapestries made of gold thread. Every dish was delivered on a gold platter, while jousting entertained the guests outside. In 1468, on the occasion of his marriage to Margaret of York, Duke Charles the Bold put on a vast pageant, which is re-enacted to this day. Sorrow began to shroud the palace after the violent death of Charles in 1477. After his daughter Mary died just five years later, the palace – and Bruges – fell from favour. The Habsburgs put it up for sale in 1631, and it passed into the hands of a Franciscan order, before

Detail from the Carmelite Church

being largely destroyed under French rule at the end of the 18th century.

MINSTRELS' CHAPEL

Leave Prinsenhof at the northwest, turning right on Ontvangersstraat, then left along Moerstraat. At the end, turn right across the canal into Beenhouwersstraat. On the left side north of the bridge is the former **Minstrels' Guild Chapel** (Speelmanskapel), built in 1421 and now owned by a private foundation, used for cultural events.

HOF SEBRECHTS PARK

A gateway in the wall on the right of Beenhouwersstraat leads into **Hof**

> ## Golden Tree Pageant
>
> The Golden Tree Pageant (Praalstoet van de Gouden Boom) recalls the festivities held during Charles the Bold's marriage to Margaret of York in 1468. After a wedding ceremony conducted in Damme, the duke paraded his bride into Bruges to enjoy days of feasting and tournaments. Named after the prize awarded to the winner of the tournament on the occasion, the pageant evokes the lives of the counts of Flanders and dukes of Burgundy, followed by a re-enactment of the wedding procession. Held every five years since 1958, usually in late August, the next pageant is in 2017.

Sebrechts Park ❸ (Mon–Fri 9am–dusk, Sat–Sun and hols 10am–dusk), a tranquil oasis behind houses. The tranquil park was originally the vegetable garden of the Sisters of St Elisabeth Convent, which stood nearby from the 15th to the 18th centuries. The park takes its name from Joseph Sebrechts, a surgeon at Sint-Janshospitaal (now the Memling Museum), who bought the property in 1928 and hired a landscape architect to create the garden. Now a public park, it has a sandpit and children's play area and, in summer, a sculpture exhibition.

Exit the park on Oude Zak. The following section of the route doesn't cover any essential sights, but it does offer a pleasant detour via another small garden to a city gate. To shorten the walk, continue to the end of Oude Zak, then turn right to cross the canal and right again to St James's Church.

PASTOR VAN HAECKE GARDEN

For the longer walk, turn left from Oude Zak onto Rozendal, a residential street in a quarter of Bruges that few tourists explore. At the end, turn right, then left on Raamstraat. This appears to be a dead end, but a gate in the wall leads into a shady **garden ❹** named after Pastor Van Haecke (1829–1912). This curate of the Basilica of the Holy Blood and sacristan of St James's Church caused controversy and was accused of Satanism. The garden is densely planted with trees and shrubs around a small pond. Exit through

Golden Tree Pageant

the gate on the eastern side to emerge onto Ezelstraat (Donkey Street).

EZELSTRAAT

Turn left and walk to the **Ezelpoort** ❺ (Donkey Gate), which dates from 1369–70 but has been frequently rebuilt since. Return towards the city and walk south on Ezelstraat. Set back from the street on the tiny Achiel van Ackerplein is the Joseph Ryelandtzaal, where a ghostly sculpture of a conductor's hands protrudes from the wall.

Carmelite Church

Further down the street, at No. 28, is the 15th-century **Carmelite Church** ❻ (Karmelietenkerk), attached to the priory of Discalced (or 'Barefoot') Carmelite Fathers that has occupied the former **Hof van Uitkerke** here since 1633. They were expelled by the French in 1795 but returned in the 19th century, and the church is one of the few places in Bruges still used by a religious order. Every Sun at 10am there is a sung Gregorian mass. Its peaceful Baroque interior (1688–91) is lined with confessionals.

ST JAMES'S CHURCH

Continue over **Ezelbrug** (Donkey Bridge) and follow the road round to the right. Just after the bend, but entered via its west door, is **St James's Church** ❼ (Sint-Jacobskerk; Apr–Sept Mon–Sat 10am–noon, 2–5pm, Sun 2–5pm),

once the richest parish church in Bruges. Built from 1220, the church grew in the 15th century thanks to generous donations from its wealthy parishioners: the Burgundian court and other merchants and courtiers. Little of its medieval character is visible today, as the interior is dominated by Baroque features added in the late 17th and early 18th centuries. However, each of the 18 altars was sponsored by a trade guild or corporation; note Lancelot Blondeel's 1523 altarpiece for the Surgeons' and Barbers' Corporation.

Return to Sint-Jakobsstraat, where refreshment options are **Wereldcafé de Republiek** and **In Den Wittenkop**, see ❶ and ❷. Head south back to Eiermarkt.

Food and Drink

❶ WERELDCAFÉ DE REPUBLIEK
Sint-Jakobsstraat 36; tel: 050 34 02 29; www.derepubliek.be; daily 11am–late; €
The arty café of the Cultuurhuis de Republiek has a large interior courtyard and does fresh food prepared up to 11pm.

❷ IN DEN WITTENKOP
Sint-Jakobsstraat 14; tel: 050 33 20 59; www.indenwittenkop.be; Tue–Sat 6–9.30pm; €€
Lined with retro advertising panels, this bistro does French fare and Belgian standards such as *waterzooï* – made with langoustines rather than white fish or chicken. Lovely terrace to the rear.

Café life on 't Zand

AROUND T'ZAND

Set out from the striking Concert Hall for this short circular route around a neighbourhood dotted with whitewashed almshouses, a chapel for the blind and a lush stretch of the ring canal.

DISTANCE: 1.5km (1 mile)
TIME: 1 hour
START/END: 't Zand
POINTS TO NOTE: This route covers an area between the station and 't Zand, where the tourist office is situated (on the ground floor of the Concert Hall). It can easily be appended to either route 2 or route 10, joining on at their nearest points.

This segment of Bruges is separated from the city centre, sandwiched between the ring road and the perimeter canal.

The hinge that keeps it connected is the 't Zand (Sand Square), site of the original railway station. Today it is dominated by the modern, terracotta-red Concert Hall, where the acoustics and musical programme are as remarkable as the architecture. To its west is a typical residential neighbourhood that is ideal for a stroll and allows you to explore a small chapel, park and almshouses.

'T ZAND

A square used for jousts, executions and tournaments from its earliest days, **'t Zand** is a focal point on the edge of the city, enlivened by funfairs, a Saturday market, the tourist office and cafés and restaurants frequented more by locals than tourists, such as **'t Putje**, see ❶.

The ring road has been buried beneath ground in recent years, allowing the once dreary square a new burst of life and to be reclaimed as a pleasant public space.

Sculpture fountain

In the centre stands a remarkable bronze **sculpture fountain ❶** (1985–86) by artists Stefaan Depuydt and Livia Canestraro. The figures depict four themes: cycling; the polder landscapes of Flanders, especially the village of Damme; fishermen, to signify the city's dependence on the sea; and four bathing women symbolising the cloth towns of Bruges, Ghent, Antwerp and Kortrijk.

Sculpture fountain on the square

Concert Hall

A striking example of contemporary architecture in a city that thrives on the past, the **Concert Hall ②** (Concertgebouw; tel: 050 47 69 99; www.concertgebouw.be; open during performances) was designed by Paul Robberecht and Hilde Daem to mark the city's year as European Capital of Culture in 2002. The exterior is clad in 68,000 terracotta tiles, a nod to the red-brick architecture of medieval Bruges. The interior is minimalistic, with bare concrete walls, and a particularly original Chamber Music Hall, where the audience sits in single rows arranged vertically in a square spiral around the stage. Known especially for its early music repertoire, the concert hall also programmes contemporary dance and new music.

On the top floor, the **Sound Factory** (Tue–Sun 9.30am–5pm; charge) is a museum space offering visitors the chance to experiment with different sound installations, including the old bells from the Belfry Tower, whilst admiring one of the best views of the city.

The **In&Uit Tourist Office** (www.brugge.be; daily 10am–5pm, Sun until 2pm) is situated in a ground-floor wing of the concert hall, as is an airy café, the **Concertgebouw-café**, see ②.

OUR LADY OF THE BLIND

Follow the shopping street of Smedenstraat west. The fourth street on the right, Kreupelenstraat, leads to a quaint chapel, **Our Lady of the Blind ③** (Onze-Lieve-Vrouw van Blindekens; Kreupelenstraat; daily 9am–5pm). Founded to honour a promise made at the battle of Monsen Pévèle in 1304 against the French (which resulted in a treaty granting Flemish independence), the church

The terracotta tiles of the Concert hall

dates from the 17th century. Its most precious artefact is a gilded 14th-century statue of the *Madonna and Child*, above a side altar. The chapel is the departure point for the annual Feast of the Assumption procession, every 15 August, to Our Lady of the Pottery on Potterierei (see page 65).

Take the alley alongside the chapel towards Kammakersstraat and peep into the neat courtyard gardens of the Van Pamel, Marius Voet and Laurentia Soutieu almshouses *(godshuizen)*, built for the blind.

BLACKSMITH'S GATE

Back on Smedenstraat, walk west to reach the **Smedenpoort** ❹ (Blacksmith's Gate), built in 1367–8 and with 17th-century modifications. The bronze skull recalls the Ghent citizen who betrayed Bruges in 1688 by trying to open the gate to French invaders, led by Louis XIV.

NIEUW WATERHUIS

Turn south on the city side of the bridge into the park that follows the line of the former ramparts, parallel to Hendrik Consciencelaan. The small brick building in the park is the **New Water House** ❺ (Nieuw Waterhuis), a pumping station used from the 14th to the 18th centuries, when a horse-actioned pump distributed drinking water across town.

BOEVERIESTRAAT

At the end of the park, head north up Boeveriestraat, lined with former almshouses, some dating from the 14th century. The **De Moor Almshouse** at Nos 52–76 was founded in 1480 for aged stonemasons, carpenters and coopers; while **Van Volden Almshouse** at No. 50 occupies the site of a medieval hospital for foundlings and mentally ill children.

Near the top on the right at Nos 5–19 are the tiny 15th-century Van Campen, Van Peenen and Gloribus (17th century) almhouses, which look too small to be inhabited by anyone but hobbits.

Food and Drink

❶ 'T PUTJE

't Zand 31; tel: 050 33 28 47; www.hotel putje.be; daily 8.30am–11pm; €€
Facing the Concert Hall, the crisp tablecloths and smart wicker chairs set this hotel brasserie apart from the nearby run-of-the-mill pavement cafés. Reliable French and Belgian classics.

❷ CONCERTGEBOUWCAFÉ

't Zand 34; tel: 050 47 69 99; www.concert gebouw.be; Wed–Sat and before and after performances, 11am–late; €
This pitstop on the ground floor of the concert hall is ideal for a straightforward, filling lunch. The sound system samples highlights from the month's programme.

Cycling along the Damme Canal

DAMME

The pretty village of Damme, 7km (4 miles) northeast of Bruges, was a major trading outpost in the Middle Ages. Hire a bike or walk up the tree-lined Damme Canal (Damse Vaart) for an easy half-day excursion.

DISTANCE: 1.25km (0.75 miles)
TIME: A half day
START: Town Hall
END: Old ramparts
POINTS TO NOTE: To get to Damme, 7km (4 miles) northeast of Bruges, either cycle or walk up the Damme Canal from Dampoort or take No. 43 bus from Bruges ('t Zand, Station or Markt; daily with exceptions in winter; 20 mins). The paddle steamer Lamme Goedzak (Apr–mid-Oct; www.bootdamme-brugge.be; 35 mins) departs just north of Dampoort at Norweegse Kaai 31; up to 5 trips a day.

Damme rose to prominence when a coastal flood and tidal wave in 1134 enlarged the Zwin inlet and permitted sea-going vessels to sail to here. A canal was dug to Bruges, and Damme became the city's main outer port, where ships moved their cargoes onto smaller boats to enter the city.

As the village grew, it enjoyed affluence and patronage. When French King Philippe-Auguste captured and razed the town in 1213, his fleet of 1,700 ships could be contained in the harbour. The town was quickly recaptured by the Flemish and a building period began, including the first fortifications. Damme remained a strategic stronghold for centuries after the sea channel silted up in 1280, when the port relocated upstream to Sluis. A second city wall was built in the 15th century.

In recent years, the village has reinvented itself as a book village. Its picturesque canalside setting, popular with strollers and cyclists, makes it a favourite destination for a Sunday lunch jaunt; thus, in addition to bookshops, Damme has many restaurants.

TOWN HALL

Begin on the main **Marktplein** (Market Square), where the diminutive **Town Hall ❶** (Stadhuis; not open to the public) was rebuilt in 1464 and has remained largely intact since. The facade niches contain figures such as Joan, Countess of Flanders (1199–1244), who gave

Herring Market

permission for the Stadhuis to be built, and Charles the Bold and Margaret of York, who married here in 1468. The belltower contains 25 bells, a sundial and a clock from 1459. On a fine day, the south-facing terrace of **Pallieter** next door is tempting, see ●.

As well as several bookshops, a Book Market is located on Marktplein in front of the Town Hall every second Sunday of the month. Damme's earliest known literary connection is celebrated on the same square – the statue here is of Jacob van Maerlant (1230–96), the 'father of Dutch poetry', who lived in Damme from around 1270 and wrote his most important works here.

TIJL UILENSPIEGEL MUSEUM

On the southeastern side of the square, the 15th-century house **De Grote Sterre** was home to Spanish governors during the 17th century; today, it contains the **Tourist Office** and **Visitor Centre** (Jacob van Maerlantstraat 3; www.toerismedamme.be; Apr–Sept Mon–Fri 9am–6pm, Sat–Sun 10am–noon, 2–6pm, Oct–Mar until 5pm and Sat–Sun 2–5pm). Also here, the **Tijl Uilenspiegel Museum** (as Tourist Office; charge)

is devoted to the 14th-century German folk-tale character Uilenspiegel, who has been adopted by the town as a mascot. In an 1867 novel by Charles De Coster, Uilenspiegel is born in Damme and leads the resistance against the Spanish occupiers.

HERRING MARKET

Walk east on Jacob van Maerlantstraat, then turn right on Corneliestraat. Opposite the junction, **De Lieve** (see page 114), is one of the town's best restaurants. Corneliestraat leads to the former **Herring Market** ❷ (Haringmarkt), where a reputed 28 million herring were processed annually in the 15th century

Church of Our Lady   *Aerial view of the village*

– hard to imagine in this tranquil square, bordered by whitewashed houses.

ST JOHN'S HOSPITAL

Retrace your steps a little, taking the first left, Pottenbakkersstraat, to reach Kerkstraat, the main road through the village. **St John's Hospital Museum** ❸ (Museum Sint-Janshospitaal; www.ocmw-damme.be; Apr–Sept Mon and Fri 2–6pm, Tue–Thur and Sat–Sun 11am–noon, 2–6pm; charge) stands at No. 33. Endowed in 1249 by Margaret of Constantinople as a hospice, and financed by the town's income from a tax on wine, the main building is Gothic, but other parts are of a later date. The museum, in the chapel and infirmary, contains furniture, paintings, silverware, documents and other items chronicling daily life in Damme.

Tante Marie, see ❷, at No. 38, is good for a snack or light meal.

CHURCH OF OUR LADY

Continue south along Kerkstraat to a path on the right leading between pollarded trees to the part-ruined **Church of Our Lady** 4 (Onze-Lieve-Vrouwekerk; May–Sept 10.30am–noon and 2.30–5.30pm), a Gothic edifice from c.1340. Climb the **tower** (charge) for a view over the village, fortifications and surrounding polder. Continue through the churchyard to exit on Burgstraat, which loops back to rejoin Kerkstraat. Walk back northwest past the Marktplein. On the way are **De Damse Poort**, see page 113, and **De Drie Zilveren Kannen** (see page 114).

OLD RAMPARTS

Damme remained a military fortress centuries after the decline of Bruges. It was on the frontline of the war between the Spanish and Dutch in the 16th and 17th centuries, and the Spanish fortifications, in the shape of a seven-point star, are still discernible. Most of the moats were filled in during building of the Damme Canal under Napoleon. See what remains by crossing the bridge and turning right. The **Nature Reserve** ❺ on the left has a path that leads among the **old ramparts**.

Food and Drink

❶ PALLIETER

Kerkstraat 12; tel: 050 35 46 75; www.pallieterdamme.be; Tue–Thur and Sat–Sun summer noon–9.30pm, winter until 7pm; €
Cosy historic restaurant with a great terrace is people watching.

❷ TANTE MARIE

Kerkstraat 38; tel: 050 35 45 03; www.tante-marie.be; Sat–Thur 10am–7pm; €
This country-style tearoom and restaurant serves great pastries and light meals.

Ostende's Flemish name

OSTEND

Leave the foreign tourists in Bruges and join the Belgians in the country's most popular seaside resort, reached in just 10 minutes by train from Bruges. It has a vast beach, fine seafood restaurants, museums and endless bustle.

DISTANCE: 5km (3 miles)
TIME: A full day
START: Museum Ship *Amandine*
END: *Mercator*
POINTS TO NOTE: A combined train-and-bike ticket from Bruges will cover the return fare and bike hire from Ostend Station, a good option out of season when the promenades are empty and you want to whisk from one attraction to another. Trains to the coast get extremely busy on fine days and in holiday periods: arrive early to get a seat. The Tourist Office (see page 128) offers a City Pass valid for one year for entry to local museums and attractions, and represents a good saving if you plan to visit several paying sights.

A former fortified town, Ostend transformed from a major fishing port to a chic holiday resort with the advent of the railways in the 19th century, when it was favoured by Belgian royalty and wealthy foreign tourists. The British frequented Ostend en masse during its 19th-century heyday, arriving in ferries from Dover to play lawn tennis, golf and beach croquet. In the 1860s Britons numbered 2,000 out of the town's total population of 16,000. The English Church, founded in the 1780s, was consecrated in its current location on Langestraat in 1865, complete with royal pew for the occasions when Queen Victoria visited her uncle King Leopold I. War damage and the demands of modern tourism erased much of its *belle époque* charm, but recent efforts to restore its image are paying off. Its good train links, cultural life, lively shopping and restaurant scene make it one of the most popular places for day-trippers and holidaymakers.

MUSEUM SHIP AMANDINE

The green-hulled fishing trawler sunk in a dry dock opposite the railway station is the **Museum Ship *Amandine* ❶** (Vindictivelaan 35; tel: 059 23 43 01; daily 10am–5pm; charge). It's a fascinating evocation of life aboard a trawler, as

Fresh from the fish market   *The beach huts on the seafront*

experienced by generations of Ostend men on perilous voyages to abundant Arctic fishing grounds. Iceland eventually extended its territorial waters and put an end to their adventures; the *Amandine* was the last such trawler to be decommissioned, in 1995.

VISSERSKAAI

Walk up the quayside of **Fishermen's Wharf** (Visserskaai), a place of pilgrimage for its fish restaurants, seafood stalls and fish market. During the early morning trawlers dock along the quay and unload crates of ice-covered fish for restaurateurs and market traders. Herring gulls line the dock and seize any chance they get (beware the fines for anyone caught feeding them). Whether now or later, be sure to try a steaming whelk *(wullok)* soup from one of the stalls. Alternatively, have a leisurely dinner in one of the many good restaurants up here, such as **Le Grillon**, see ❶.

Fish Market
A little further up on the right, the utilitarian concrete block on the quayside houses the stalls of the **Fish Market ❷** (Vistrap), open from 6 or 7am each day to sell the night's catch. Early birds can watch as crates of sole, cod, haddock and halibut are winched up from fishing boats that dock alongside. Fish doesn't come fresher than this, although prices here are rather tourist-focused.

AROUND LANGESTRAAT

Turn left into Langestraat, which runs west to the casino. At No. 101 is the **English Church**.

Museum of Local History
The first royal palace on the Belgian coast, at No. 69, is more bourgeois home than castle; it provides a fine setting for the **Ostend History Museum 'De Plate' ❸** (Oostends Historisch Museum 'De Plate'; www.deplate.be; Wed–Mon 10am–12.30pm, 2–6pm; charge). Inside 'the plaice' (as it is nicknamed) is a well-displayed collection of artefacts evoking the city's nautical past. There are model yachts and liners, reconstructions of a fishermen's café and a living room of 1900, archaeological finds, historical maps tracing the changing shape of the city, photos and paintings depicting illustrious maritime events as well as daily life at the fish market, and colourful *belle époque* posters advertising cross-Channel ferry trips. Most curious of all is the preserved death-chamber of Belgium's first queen, Louise-Marie, wife of Leopold I, who died here of tuberculosis in 1850.

James Ensor House
At Vlaanderenstraat, turn right to visit, at No. 27, the **James Ensor House ❹** (James Ensor Huis; www.muzee.be/en/muzee; Wed–Mon 10am–noon and 2–5pm; charge). The painter was

The Albert I-Promenade and Casino Kursaal

born in Ostend in 1860, and returned to live and work from 1916 until his death in 1949 above a modest souvenir shop run by his aunt and uncle. The shells, masks and curios in the shop's cabinets indicate where he may have sourced his inspiration. Upstairs, the original decor and furnishings of the living rooms have been restored. Reproductions of Ensor's artworks cover the walls, illustrating the fantastical imaginings of the artist.

Casino Kursaal

Return to Langestraat, which has some of the liveliest watering holes in town, such as **Tao Bar**, see ②. At its western end is the **Tourist Office ⑤** (Monacoplein 2; www.visitoostende. be; Oct–May 10am–6pm, June–Sept 9am–7pm), where you can pick up a useful City Pass (see page 128). Across the road stands a proud Ostend institution – the **Casino Kursaal ⑥**, a concert hall and casino with function rooms, bars and a chic restaurant on the top floor.

ALBERT I-PROMENADE

Walk around the casino and hit the promenade and main beach, having skipped a rather dull stretch of apartment blocks east of this point – the expanse of quartz sand dotted with traditional beach huts more than compensates. This is the place for pancake or ices on a terrace. Alternatively you could have something more substantial at **Beluga** (see page 114), or at family-run **Villa Borghese** (see page 114).

The colonnaded Royal Galleries

Royal Ostend

Further along the seafront are the 19th-century **Venetian Galleries** ❼ (Venetiaanse Gaanderijen). At the entrance to this former royal pavilion stands a bronze sculpture, cast in 2000, depicting the late **King Baudouin** (r.1951–93) on foot and wearing a raincoat on a visit to Ostend.

Albert I-Promenade melds into the Zeedijk (Sea Dyke). The equestrian statue on the left, created in 1931, depicts **King Leopold II** (r.1865–1909) gazing out to sea, flanked by Ostend fisherfolk and being hailed by a Congolese native. Given Leopold's brutish colonial rule over the Congo as well as his looting of its mineral wealth, the bare-faced cheek of this statue is astounding.

Continue to the colonnaded **Royal Galleries** ❽ (Koninklijke Gaanderijen), built in 1906 so that Leopold II and his court could shelter from the wind as they passed along the seafront. The Art Deco **Thermae Palace Hotel** (www. thermaepalace.be) in the centre dates back to 1933.

Turn back to the Leopold statue and pass beneath the arch to reach Koningin Astridlaan. Turn left and walk via Warschauwstraat to Leopold I-Plein and its equestrian statue of **Leopold I** (r.1831–65), first King of the Belgians.

MUSEUM BY THE SEA

Head south on Rogierlaan and sidestep into Romestraat to reach the excellent **MuZEE** ❾ (www.muzee.be/en/muzee; Tue–Sun 10am–6pm; charge). The Museum by the Sea (Kunstmuseum aan Zee) contains works by an impressive roster of Belgian artists: James Ensor, Leon Spilliaert, Paul Delvaux, Panamarenko, Jan Fabre as well as Luc Tuymans. It also hosts temporary exhibitions of international contemporary art, and the café does reasonably priced lunches and snacks.

LEOPOLDPARK

Walk north up Romestraat, cross Alfons Pieterslaan and up Leon Spilliaertstraat to the **Leopold Park** (Leopoldpark) ❿, a landscaped park with a lake and bridges, a playground for under-10s, a mini-golf course and a pleasant café. Cross the park diagonally to exit at the northern corner on Leopold II-Laan. Continue up to Marie Joseplein, where you could pause for a drink in the stylish **Brasserie du Parc**, see ❸.

WAPENPLEIN

Turn right along Adolph Buylstraat, a pedestrianised street which leads to **Wapenplein** ⓫. This square, the geographical and commercial heart of the city, is dominated by the **Belltower** (Beiaardtoren), built in 1964, which plays a tune composed by James Ensor. The adjoining building (1958), once a museum of fine arts, is now a **shopping arcade**.

Ostend's marina

CHURCH OF SS PETER AND PAUL

Take Kerkstraat south (or, if you prefer to walk past shops, parallel Kapellestraat) to the neo-Gothic **Church of SS Peter and Paul** ⑫ (Sint-Petrus-en-Pauluskerk; Sint-Petrus-en-Paulusplein; tel: 059 80 04 27; daily). Completed in 1907 by Bruges architect Louis Delacenserie, it includes a chapel (behind the choir) for the mausoleum of Queen Louise-Marie, who died in Ostend in 1850. The lovely stained-glass windows were added after World War II.

To the west stands **St Peter's Tower** (St Pieterstoren), the remainder of the very first St Peter's church (1458). The octagonal tower was added in the early 18th century and explains its nickname, De Peperbus (The Peppermill).

MARINA

Exiting the church, take Dekenijstraat south to the yacht marina, home to the three-masted schooner **Mercator** ⑬ (Mercatordok; www.zeilschip-mercator.be; daily 10am–5pm except 24, 25 and 31 Dec and 1 Jan; charge). This former merchant navy training ship once sailed as far as Easter Island; its sumptuous polished wood furnishings are a far cry from the basic quarters aboard the *Amandine*, a short walk away.

Food and Drink

① LE GRILLON

Visserskaai 31; tel: 059 70 60 63; www.legrillon.be; Fri–Tue noon–3pm, 6–10pm; €€

Poached ray wing and other classics of the French seafood repertoire are prepared at this timeless classic by three superb chefs, one of whom has been at the helm for 40 years. The food and service are formal without being stuffy.

② TAO BAR

Langestraat 24–26; tel: 059 43 83 73; www.tao-oostende.be; restaurant: Wed–Sat 5.30–10pm, Sun and hols noon–10pm; bar: Wed–Thur from 4pm, Fri–Sun from 2pm; €

This lounge, bar and fusion restaurant in the heart of the nightlife district is helping put the edge back into Ostend. The menu features Belgian, Thai, Mexican and tapas dishes, and then it's up on the dance floor for a dressed-up beach party with DJs.

③ BRASSERIE DU PARC

Marie Joseplein 3; tel: 059 51 13 05; www.brasserieduparc.be; daily from 8am; €

A beautiful Art Deco hotel-café with original fixtures and fittings and ageing intellectuals enjoying the paper and a cigarette – a gem in an otherwise post-war townscape. Breakfast and light brasserie meals are served in charmingly old-school style.

Commemorating fallen soldiers at Ypres

YPRES

The history of Ypres (Ieper in Flemish) is one of glory and tragedy. One of the largest and richest cities of medieval Europe, it became a byword for the horrors of trench warfare during World War I, and was reconstructed from ruin after 1918.

DISTANCE: Walk: 3km (2 miles); drive: 34km (21 miles)
TIME: A full day
START/END: Walk: Grote Markt; drive: Meenseweg beyond Menin Gate
POINTS TO NOTE: Ypres is 60km (37 miles) south-west of Bruges. Hourly trains connect Bruges to Ypres (at least 1.5 hours; change at Kortrijk). By car the fastest route is via the A17/E403 south to Kortrijk, taking the Moorsele exit and travelling west on the A19 to Ieper (70km/43 miles; 50 mins). Tour operators organise trips to the battlefields (see page 129). If possible, avoid the In Flanders Fields Museum on Tue, Thur and Fri in term-time, when schools visit.

Few visitors to this tranquil town are aware that in 1260 it had a population that matched London's (50,000-strong) and a reputation for weaving the finest cloth in Europe. Despite being part of France, the town sided with England in the Hundred Years War due to its dependence on English wool. It backed the wrong horse – plague, starvation and battle ensued, and by the 15th century cloth production and the population had both declined by 90 percent.

A fortress town for the next four centuries, its ramparts proved useless against the shells of World War I, when it was blasted to oblivion as German and British forces dug into trenches east of the city. Offensives from 1914–18 claimed hundreds of thousands of lives, while the lines barely shifted. After the Armistice, the town was rebuilt, complete with medieval monuments. Now affluent, it has embraced its role as a place of pilgrimage for historians and families of those who died on the Front.

GROTE MARKT

From the railway station, the city centre is about 1km (0.6 mile) on foot. Cross the road in front to Colaertplein, keeping the garden to your left. Walk down Stationstraat, turn left at the end on Tempelstraat then right on Boterstraat. Round the corner is **De Ruyffelaer** (see

Cloth Hall

page 114) but for now continue along Boterstraat to the **Grote Markt ❶**, the hub of activity in this otherwise tranquil town. Looking at the buildings, from the immense Cloth Hall and Belfry on your left to the individually designed houses, it is hard to grasp that the entire square was rebuilt to its medieval design after World War I. It is now lined with eateries, including **Old Tom** (see page 114).

Cloth Hall

The vast **Cloth Hall** (Lakenhalle) bears witness to Ypres's prominence as a medieval wool town. Longer than the cathedral (120m/394ft) and with 48 doors to the street, it was built in 1250–1378 by the River Ieperlee (now vaulted). Boats sailed into the building, which served as a storehouse and market for wool and cloth. Halfway along sits the 70m (230ft) **Belfry** (Belfort); a stump was all that remained in 1918. Next door is the **Tourist Office** (www.visitypres.be; Mon–Fri 9am–5pm, Sat–Sun 10am–5pm).

In Flanders Fields Museum

The Cloth Hall's first floor houses the excellent **In**

Flanders Fields Museum ❷ (www.inflandersfields.be; Apr–mid-Nov daily 10am–6pm, mid-Nov–Mar Tue-Sun 10am–5pm, last entry 1hr before; closed most of Jan; charge). Named after the poem by Canadian physician and poet John McCrae (1872–1918), who died on active service, the museum brings to life the conflict that claimed 550,000 lives on the Flemish front from 1914–18. Maquettes describe battles that took place for mere metres of territory over four

St Martin's Cathedral   *Menin Gate*

years along the Ypres Salient; letters, mementoes and recordings evoke the experience of trench warfare; and an audio soundscape recreates No Man's Land in chilling style.

ST MARTIN'S CATHEDRAL

Pass through the arch beneath the Belfry to reach **St Martin's Cathedral** ❸ (Sint-Maartenskathedraal; Vandepeereboomplein; daily, closed noon– 2pm and during mass). Founded in the 11th century on the site of a fortified chapel of the counts of Flanders, the Gothic church was originally built in 1221. A bishopric from 1559–1801, the church was confiscated following the French Revolution and sold for building materials, but a churchwarden managed to buy it back. The current edifice was rebuilt 1922–30, when it gained a steeple of 102m (335ft). For refreshment nearby, try **'t Ganzeke**, see ❶.

ST GEORGE'S CHURCH

At the northwestern corner of the square before the cathedral is the Anglican **St George's Memorial Church** ❹ (daily Apr–Sept 9.30am– 8pm, Oct–Mar until 4.30pm), erected in memory of British and Commonwealth soldiers who died in World War I. Furnished with donations from bereaved families, it is a moving shrine to a sacrificed generation. An attached schoolhouse, funded by Eton School to honour old boys who had died, was opened for the children of War Graves Commission staff to teach them 'English and good manners'. Today, it is the church hall.

MENIN GATE

Return to the Grote Markt and cross to the southeastern corner, taking Meensestraat to the **Menenpoort** ❺ (Menin Gate), an arch inscribed with the names of 55,000 of the 100,000 Commonwealth soldiers who died in battle before 16 August 1917 but have no known grave (those who perished later are commemorated in Tyne Cot cemetery; see page 87). At 8pm daily traffic through the gate is stopped and Ypres firefighter buglers play 'The Last Post' to remember those who died fighting for Belgium's freedom.

RAMPARTS

Climb the steps in the Menin Gate's southern side and walk south along the former city **ramparts**. Dating back to the 10th century, today they reflect the 17th-century layout created by French fortress designer Vauban for Louis XIV, providing a view of historic bastions, gates and islands. During World War I, sleeping quarters and hospitals were set up in tunnels within the ramparts (accessible only by guided tour).

The former city ramparts

Ramparts Cemetery

Continue to **Lille Gate** ❻ (Rijselpoort), the oldest city gate, built under Burgundian rule in the 14th century. Just beyond, by the water, is the **Ramparts Cemetery** ❼, where the 193 Allied graves include members of the Maori Battalion, Canadian Engineers, Royal Irish Rifles and Essex Regiment.

CITY MUSEUM

Turn back towards town and walk up Ieperleestraat, parallel to and west of busy Rijselsestraat. A rare historic building to have survived the 1914–18 bombardments, **St John's Almshouse** (Sint-Jansgodshuis) at No. 31 was an institution for the poor from 1270. Today, it houses the **City Museum** ❽ (Stedelijk Museum; Tue–Sun 10am–12.30pm, 2–6pm, Nov–Mar until 5pm; charge, or included in In Flanders Fields Museum ticket). Paintings from the 18th and 19th centuries illustrate the 'lost' Ypres, a film explains the city's turbulent past, and there's a focus on Louise De Hem (1866–1922), a local artist who braved social disapproval to pursue her career in a man's world.

To rejoin the Grote Markt, turn right twice and then left along Rijselsestraat.

YPRES SALIENT

If you have your own transport, the following circuit visits principal World War I sites out of town. Take the road to Menen beyond the gate. Follow Zonnebeekseweg for a short distance, then turn right on Meenseweg (N8). After about 3km (2 miles), turn right on Canadalaan, where there are signs for Sanctuary Wood and Hill 62.

Sanctuary Wood and Hill 62

Sanctuary Wood Museum (Canadalaan 26; daily 10am–6pm; charge) is owned by the family of the original farmer. Its collection of armaments, shells, 3D photographs and uniforms is unlabelled, but the highlight, in a patch of adjoining woodland, is one of the few remaining sections of trench lines.

Continue a short walk up the road to **Hill 62**, the Canadian memorial (62m/38ft above sea level) marking the site

---

Cat parade

One of Belgium's more bizarre folk festivals takes place in Ypres every three years on the second Sunday in May (the next in 2015). The Kattenstoet (Cat Parade) recalls the medieval tradition of hurling live cats from the top of the Belfry to ward off evil spirits, a practice maintained until 1817 (and revived between the world wars). The costumed procession of 2,000 participants, horses, giants and floats, evokes the symbolism of the cat in history and folklore. It culminates with the cat-throwing (soft toys only) and a 'witch-burning' party.

WWI trenches at Hill 62   *Tyne Cot Cemetery*

of fierce fighting in 1916 by Canadian troops defending the southern stretch of the Ypres Salient.

Passchendaele Museum
Return to the N8, turn left towards Ypres and then immediately right on narrow Begijnenbosstraat. This cuts the corner to reach the N37, where you should turn right towards Zonnebeke. At the centre in Zonnebeke Château is the **Memorial Museum Passchendaele 1917** (Feb–Nov daily 9am–5pm; www.passchendaele.be; charge), recounting the bloody Third Battle of Ypres in dioramas, photos and film, plus a reconstructed dugout.

Tyne Cot
Continue through Zonnebeke to the suburb of Broodseinde, turn left on the N303 for about 1km (0.6 mile) and then left (follow signs) to **Tyne Cot Cemetery**, the world's largest Commonwealth cemetery. The most potent reminder of Passchendaele, it honours the victims of 100 days' fighting for a gain of barely 8km (5 miles): 245,000 British and 215,000 German troops. The **Visitor Centre** (Feb–Nov daily 10am–6pm) evokes their stories.

German Soldiers' Cemetery
Return to Zonnebeke and turn right at the roundabout. At the N313 turn right then immediately left to Langemark and right at the church. As you exit the village, the **German Soldiers' Cemetery** (Deutscher Soldatenfriedhof) is on the left, the only German war cemetery on the Ypres Salient. From the car park just beyond the cemetery, follow the audiovisual presentation on the path to the cemetery, a sombre place in pink sandstone and granite beneath oak trees. Buried here are 44,000 soldiers, many of them members of Student Regiments. Around 15 percent of Germany's volunteer corps raised at the outbreak of the war was students and high-school graduates, many recruited in entire classes with their professors. On 24 October 1914 the enthusiastic but untrained volunteers were sent marching at Langemark towards the only professional army in Europe, the British Expeditionary Force (BEF). They died in their thousands, prompting the Germans to remember the battle as the 'massacre of the innocents at Ypres' ('Kindermord bei Ypern').

From Langemark, return to the N313, turning right to go straight back to Ypres.

Food and Drink

1 'T GANZEKE

Vandepeereboomplein 5; tel: 057 20 00 09; Tue–Thu 9am–10.30pm, Fri–Sat until 11.30pm; €

This tavern and tearoom, decorated with model geese, serves tasty snacks and full meals round the clock.

Busy Graslei

GHENT

Vibrant, historic Ghent is 20 minutes by train from Bruges. While the city may lack the latter's picture-postcard prettiness, it does have at least as many sights and a lively urban edge thanks to a large student population.

> **DISTANCE:** 2.5km (1.5 miles)
> **TIME:** A full day
> **START:** St Nicholas Church
> **END:** St Michael's Church
> **POINTS TO NOTE:** As in Bruges, most museums in Ghent close on a Monday. However, the two big sights, St Bavo's and the Castle of the Counts, do open then. There are frequent trains from Bruges to Gent-Sint-Pieters Station. On arrival, head to the tram stop under the bridge to the left as you exit the station and take tram No. 1 to Korenmarkt in the centre. Avoid walking, as the route is long and uninteresting. If coming by car, take the E40.

Over twice the size of Bruges and with more dispersed sites, Ghent, on the confluence of the Leie and Scheldt rivers, grew rich on its cloth industry and the import of grain, and was prized by the counts of Flanders and dukes of Burgundy. This circuit concentrates on the historic centre, where there is plenty to see within a small radius, includ-ing one of the finest paintings in West-ern art, the van Eyck altarpiece, in the cathedral. A longer visit can be reward-ing, as Ghent has two fine art museums towards its periphery and a lively cul-tural scene. The youthful demographic means the city has many more budget options for dining out than in Bruges and some seriously good nightlife.

ST NICHOLAS CHURCH

Alight from the tram at Korenmarkt and **St Nicholas Church ❶** (Sint-Niklaaskerk; www.stniklaas.com; Mon 2–5pm, Tue–Sun 10am–5pm). The 13th-century church in Scheldt Gothic style was founded by the city's Tradesmen's Guild. It suffered centuries of neglect, start-ing with stability problems in the 16th century, yet has survived repeated calls for demolition. Works begun in 1957 have reached the nave; the transept, choir and ambulatory are open and have been restored to their Gothic austerity – unlike the Baroque altar and other dec-oration added in the 17th century when the western portal was built (visible from outside). Properties built against the church's northern facade on Klein Turkije give an idea of how the entire exterior used to appear.

BELFRY

Walk east from St Nicholas to Sint-Baaf-splein, where church and city authorities faced each other across the square. The **Belfry ❷** (Belfort; www.visitgent. be; daily 10am–6pm; charge) was completed in 1380 following the guilds' entry onto the town council. The tower, at 91m (299ft) tall, was intended as a symbol of the guilds' power – the charter detailing the rights and privileges of the people was stored in a strongroom here, while the bells took over from churches the task of informing citizens at what time to get up and go to work. Originally, there was just one large bell (the Roeland bell from 1377), which rang hourly; a smaller chiming set was added later. The melody of the quarter-hourly chime is changed every two years just before Easter Sunday. Although less impressive to climb than the belfry in Bruges, at least this one has a lift. A guided tour is available in Dutch and English every day at 3.30pm.

Cloth Hall

Ghent, like Bruges, made its fortune from weaving cloth, which was valued, examined and sold in the 1441 **Cloth Hall** (Lakenhalle) next to the Belfry. An annexe (1741) to the Cloth Hall's west-ern facade was used as the guard's quarters when the hall served as a jail. This is known as The Suckler (De Mam-melokker), after the sculpture above the doorway showing Roman Charity: Cimon being suckled by his daughter Pero, a wet-nurse.

ST BAVO'S CATHEDRAL

Facing the Belfry on the eastern side of Sint-Baafsplein is **St Bavo's Cathe-dral ❸** (Sint-Baafskathedraal; Apr–Oct Mon–Sat 8.30am–6pm, Sun 1–6pm, Nov–Mar until 5pm, Sun 1–5pm). A mix of sombre high Gothic and flamboyant late Gothic style, built during the 14th–16th centuries, the church started out as plain St John's, founded in the 10th century and the first parish church in Ghent. In 1559 it gained cathedral status and a dedication to the 7th-century Flemish saint St Bavo. The cavernous interior is rich in treasures, most notably the *Mystic Lamb* altarpiece. Other highlights include the Rubens altarpiece (1624), in which the artist portrays himself as St Bavo, and Frans Pourbus the Elder's *Jesus among the Scribes* (1571), the cast of which includes Emperor Charles V, his son King Philip II of Spain and the artist Pieter Brueghel the Elder. The Baroque high altar (1719) is a triumph of pomp in white, black and red-flamed marble, while the Baroque organ (1653) is the largest in Benelux, with 7,000 pipes. Among many other artworks, the series

St Bavo's lofty interior

of bishop portraits from the 16th century to the present makes for a fascinating study of ecclesiastical fashions. Since spring 2013, the cathedral tower has been under scaffolding, undergoing a major overhaul (this could last for four years).

Mystic Lamb

Belgium's greatest art treasure alone justifies the trip to Ghent: **The Adoration of the Mystic Lamb** (1432), or the Ghent Altarpiece, by the brothers Jan and Hubert van Eyck. The 20-panel polyptych marked a turning point for painting and religious art, blending Gothic ideals of abstraction and mysticism with the realism and naturalism that characterised the Renaissance. Although designed for the cathedral's Vijdt chapel (beyond the high altar), it is displayed in the **former baptismal chapel** (Mon–Sat 9.30am–5pm, Sun and hols 1–5pm, Nov–Mar 10.30am–4pm; charge), to the left of the door as you enter.

The altarpiece was commissioned by wealthy alderman Judocus Vijdt and his wife; their portraits appear on the back panels of the closed polyptych. The childless couple chose the Annunciation theme, and the artist included esoteric symbols that would have been appreciated by the patron and Philip the Good, duke of Burgundy. Among the 200 figures depicted, there are references to Virgil, Jewish texts, Byzantium and science. One panel – the 'Just Judges', on the lower left – was stolen in 1934 and a ransom note sent to the bishop. It has never been recovered. A five-year restoration programme started in 2012 and although the Ghent Altarpiece itself remains on view, some panels may not be on show.

Detail from 'The Adoration of the Mystic Lamb'

VRIJDAGMARKT

Exit St Bavo's and take Biezekapel-straat to your right. Cross Hoogpoort and continue down Zandberg. For lunch here, try **De Warempel**, see ➊.

Head straight on, then turn left at the end to face **St James's Church** (Sint-Jacobskerk). Walk around the church and straight on to reach **Vrijdagmarkt ➍**, named after the Friday market held here since the 13th century. Bordered by guildhouses and mansions, the square has been the scene of jousting tournaments, executions and political skirmishes; now bordered by cafés, it is liveliest at night. **Dulle Griet**, see ➋, has the best beer selection.

Jacob van Artevelde Statue

The **statue** (1863) on the square commemorates textiles merchant and brewer Jacob van Artevelde (c.1290–1345), who in 1338, in the Hundred Years War between France and England, rallied Ghent's merchants and guilds in support of England's King Edward III against the count of Flanders. Seven years later, he was assassinated on Vrijdagmarkt at a riot between weavers and wool-makers after suggesting that Edward the Black Prince, son of Edward III, should be made count of Flanders.

Guildhouses

The square's most striking house is the **Tanners' Guildhouse** (Gildehuis van de Huidevetters) on the corner of Kammer-straat. Built 1450–83, it was the meeting place for the weavers' quality commission, who would shame poor-quality work by hanging bolts of linen or cloth from its Little Tower (Toreken).

Socialist headquarters

On the opposite side of the square, the Art Nouveau edifice **Our House** (Ons Huis) was the headquarters of the Socialist workers' association, built in 1899. Its gold inscription, in Dutch, reads 'Workers of World Unite'.

PATERSHOL DISTRICT

Leave Vrijdagmarkt via Grootkanon-plein and cross the bridge. The streets behind Kraanlei quayside form **Patershol ➎**, where renovation has transformed this former red-light district of 17th-century houses into a hip quarter with boutiques, bars and restaurants. The city has made a keen effort to preserve the residential character of the neighbourhood, which was once home to tanners and weavers, and there are strict rules regulating the number of businesses here.

Folklore Museum

Walk south down Kraanlei to no. 65, the **Folkore Museum ➏** (Huis van Alijn; www.huisvanalijn.be; Tue–Sat 11am–5pm, Sun 10am–5pm; charge). Located in a former children's hospital, it displays a collection of artefacts pertaining to birth, illness, marriage and

Folklore Museum

death rituals, the evolution of leisure time, and traditional crafts and trades. A projection room showing 'found footage' from home movies, and a 'speaking chamber', with recordings of the various Flemish dialects, are both fascinating. The Huis van Alijn almshouse was founded in 1363 in reparation for a family feud. In 1354 a girl named Godelieve chose to marry Hendrik Alijn instead of her intended, Simeon Rijm. In revenge, Rijm killed Alijn and his brother. As punishment, the Rijm family homes were demolished, and Simeon was ordered to build an almshouse on land donated by the Alijns. The original was replaced in 1519.

CASTLE OF THE COUNTS

At the end of Kraanlei, turn right to Sint-Veerleplein and the **Castle of the Counts** ❼ (Gravensteen; www.visitgent. be; daily Apr–Sept 10am–6pm, Oct–Mar 9am–5pm; charge). Built by the counts of Flanders in the 11th century, the castle was used, successively, as a fortress, administrative centre and court of justice (14th–18th centuries), and factory and workers' residence (19th century). The visit to the battlements and keep culminates in a room containing gruesome torture instruments.

DESIGN MUSEUM

Walk west, cross the bridge, then turn south into Jan Breydelstraat. At No. 5,

the Hotel De Coninck houses the **Design Museum Gent** ❽ (www.designmuseum gent.be; Tue–Sun 10am–6pm; charge), with 17th- and 18th-century furniture in the front house and a superb Art Nouveau collection in the modern wing, plus furniture from the 1970s and 80s. Built in 1755, the former family mansion was furnished in the height of luxury before its owner's wedding. The panelled dining room is original, embellished with motifs to love and marriage, with an ornate Baroque chandelier in carved oak. After so much visual stimulus, the **Brooderie** bakery-café opposite will be a welcome stop, see ❸.

KORENLEI AND GRASLEI

Jan Breydelstraat brings you to the city's commercial centre during the 11th–18th centuries. The stretch of the River Leie known as 'Tussen Bruggen' (Between the Bridges) formed a harbour, flanked with guildhouses and warehouses. Many buildings here were renovated for the 1913 Ghent World Fair, not always with great attention to historical accuracy, but the effect is still stunning; the broad quaysides still buzz with activity on a fine day, although beer-drinking students have replaced haggling merchants.

On the western bank is **Korenlei** ❾ (Grass Quay), with the renovated 16th-century **The Swan** (De Swane) at No. 9. The former brewery is now a Marriott hotel. At No. 7, the **Guildhouse**

Castle of the Counts   *St Michael's church and bridge*

of the **Tied Boatmen**, known as The Anchor (Den Ancker), was built in 1739. Tied Boatmen were not permitted to unload their cargo within the city limits, and had to tranship their loads onto the vessels of the Free Boatmen.

On **Graslei ⑩** (Herb Quay), opposite, the late-12th-century Romanesque **Corn Stockpile House** (Het Spijker) at No. 9 was used to store grain until 1734. Its Tournai limestone facade contains what is thought to be the oldest step gable in the country. Next door, at No. 11, is the Flemish Renaissance **Little Customs House** (Tolhuisje), where duties were paid on grain stored. Nos 12–13 were the **Corn Measurer's House** (Korenmetershuis or Coorenmetershuys), a Gothic building from 1540 with Baroque gable (1698). No. 14 is the **Guildhouse of the Free Boatmen** (Gildenhuis van de Vrije Schippers), built in 1355 with a facade from 1531.

ST MICHAEL'S CHURCH

Graslei brings you to **St Michael's Bridge** (1910), with fine views north over the river and east to Ghent's three great towers. To the west of the bridge stands **St Michael's Church ⑪** (Sint-Michielskerk; Apr–Sept Mon–Sat 2–5pm), which was commissioned by the Brewers' Guild in 1440, but never got a tower due to lack of funds. Inside, the space seems immense, with many side chapels. Artworks include *Christ on the Cross* (1630) by Anthony van Dyck.

Food and Drink

① DE WAREMPEL
Zandberg 8; tel: 09 224 30 62; Mon–Fri 11.45am–2pm, Fri also 6–9pm; €
The menu at this vegetarian lunch restaurant and local favourite comprises a one-dish mixed platter, with optional soup starter and dessert. The custom is to join a table with other diners.

② DULLE GRIET
Vrijdagmarkt 50; tel: 09 224 24 55; www.dullegriet.be; Mon 4.30pm–1am, Tue–Sat noon–1am, Sun noon–7.30pm; €
Behind the lace lampshades and café curtains, this old-style Flemish tavern serves 250 different beers, including Ghent's own Stropken, Gentse Tripel and Augustijnerbier, and the renowned Kwak (served in a 1.5 litre glass, for which a shoe is required as deposit).

③ BROODERIE
Jan Breydelstraat 8; tel: 09 225 06 23; www.brooderie.be; Tue–Sun 8am–6pm; €
Breakfast, lunch and afternoon teas are served on scrubbed pine tables in this homely bakery store, which also has B&B rooms upstairs. Cakes are homemade and portions are generous: the moist, dark spice cake is a local speciality.

DIRECTORY

Hand-picked hotels and restaurants to suit all budgets and tastes, organised by area, plus select nightlife listings, an alphabetical listing of practical information, a language guide and an overview of the best books and films to give you a flavour of the city.

Hotel de Orangerie occupies a lovely spot by the water

ACCOMMODATION

As a favourite destination for romantic getaways, Bruges is blessed with cosy hotels in medieval properties with canal views and period features. It presents more of a challenge to budget travellers or those looking for large rooms, a lift, gym or easy parking. Price deals vary and breakfast, if not included, is probably overpriced and worth seeking elsewhere. Be aware, too, that with canals may come a certain drainy whiff, and mosquitoes in warmer months. Pay for a view of the water if you wish, but in a city full of awesome views at every turn, you may decide this is a dispensable feature unless the hotel has air-conditioning. The majority of hotels are in the historic centre, so walking to sights is not a problem. Bus routes from the station or 't Zand are also listed.

Bed and breakfast

There are a good number of bed and breakfast options in Bruges, many in tastefully renovated homes whose owners are keen to share their city's charms. Inexpensive compared to

Price for a double room for one night including breakfast:
€€€€ = over 200 euros
€€€ = 130–200 euros
€€ = 80–130 euros
€ = below 80 euros

hotels, this option is worth considering if you don't require a mini-bar or room service, but book early as rooms are limited. Several B&B addresses are listed at www.brugge-bedandbreakfast.com (a handy map graphic gives an instant location guide) or the Tourist Office site www.brugge.be, which has a more complete list. Bookings can normally be made online, but be aware that few owners accept credit cards.

Centre

Crowne Plaza Brugge

Burg 10; tel: 050 44 68 44; www.crowne plaza.com/bruggebel; bus: 0/Centrum; €€
It's hard to forgive the town planners who allowed this featureless edifice to be built on the historic Burg square. Inside, however, you get the fabulous view out, roomy bedrooms, big beds, swish bathrooms and the details and service you would expect from a top hotel, including kettles in rooms, a rare thing in Belgium. The basement contains the ruins of St Donatian's, the former cathedral, which makes for a bizarre feature in a conference suite. Underground parking is available beneath the hotel and low-season room rates can be excellent.

Hotel de Orangerie

Kartuizerinnenstraat 10; tel: 050 34 16 49; www.hotelorangerie.be; bus: 0/Centrum; €€€€

Boat–Hotel De Barge

Situated in a narrow street close to the Belfry, the Orangerie could not be more central. A former 15th-century convent, it is a romantic choice, with the water of the Dijver canal lapping at its terrace and just 20 rooms, all prettily furnished. A stylish makeover has transformed it into a cosy boutique hotel furnished with fine antiques, a wood-panelled dining room and a lounge like a private members' club. Try to avoid ground-floor rooms facing the street. The hotel also has a lovely terrace, which is an ideal place to take the English-style afternoon tea that is served daily.

Oud Huis de Peellaert

Hoogstraat 20; tel: 050 33 78 89; www.depeellaert.com; bus: 0/Centrum; €€

A stylish hotel set in a 19th-century mansion in the heart of the old town. Inside, you'll find an artistic blend of antiques and modern details such as Alessi cutlery. The beds are comfortable and the buffet breakfast in one of the best in Bruges.

Relais Bourgondisch Cruyce

Wollestraat 41–47; tel: 050 33 79 26; www.relaisbourgondischcruyce.be; bus: 1, 6, 11, 16; €€€

A gorgeous small hotel in two gabled houses with timbered facades backing onto a canal. Decorated in sumptuous 17th-century Flemish style with carved furniture, stone floors and large fireplaces – if you've seen *In Bruges*, you'll recognise it from the film. The 16 bed-

rooms combine traditional decor with modern design. If you can, it is worth paying extra here for a canal-view room.

South

Boat-Hotel De Barge

Bargeweg 15; tel: 050 38 51 50; www.hoteldebarge.be; bus: 2, 12; €€€

Wake up to the sound of ducks outside the window in this unusual hotel located in a converted Flemish canal barge. The rooms (cabins) may be small, but they have an appealing nautical flavour, with white wood, blue paint and bright red lifejackets laid out on the beds. The hotel has a bar, terrace, restaurant and car park. Located just outside the Old Town, a brisk 10-minute walk from the centre beside a coach park (not visible) and conveniently near the railway station. At the low end of the price range.

Botaniek

Waalsestraat 23; tel: 050 34 14 24; www.botaniek.be; bus: 6, 16; €€

A homely little hotel with a warm welcome, situated between the centre and Astrid Park in a quiet neighbourhood. The nine-room establishment occupies an 18th-century townhouse furnished in Louis XV style, fresh but without pretension. Rooms on the top floor have wonderful views of gabled houses and ancient spires. There is also a small lift, rare for a characterful hotel in Bruges.

Egmond

Minnewater 15; tel: 050 34 14 45;

Grand breakfast room at Jan Brito

www.egmond.be; bus: 2, 20, 21; €€

This attractive, small hotel is located in a gabled Flemish mansion next to the romantic Minnewater lake. The interior is furnished in an appealing Flemish traditional style, complete with tiled floors, oak chests and 18th-century fireplaces. The eight bedrooms look out on a rambling garden, making for peaceful nights. There is a car park for guests, and the station is just a 10-minute walk away.

Ibis Hotel

Marie Popelinplantsoen 4; tel: 050 40 51 20; www.accorhotels.com; bus: 1, 3–9, 11, 13–17; €€

This Ibis budget hotel is adjacent to the station. The rooms are basic but clean, with television and paid-for internet access. Late arrivals can rest assured that reception is open 24/7 and that there is parking nearby. It may not be Bruges' most romantic hotel, however the location should not be underestimated – with visitors arriving by train able to immediately drop their bags off before a quick 10-minute walk to the centre. A good-value, practical option.

Jan Brito

Freren Fonteinstraat 1; tel: 050 33 06 01; www.janbrito.eu; bus: 6, 16; €€€

This 23-room hotel occupies a 16th-century merchant's house with a secluded Renaissance garden. Staff are friendly, and furnishings and decoration classic and tasteful. Room styles and prices vary enormously, from suites to the 'Maid's Room', a budget option!

't Keizershof

Oostmeers 126; tel: 050 33 87 28; www.hotelkeizershof.be; bus: 0/Centrum; €

The perfect place for anyone travelling on a tight budget, this compact, seven-room establishment is located close to the railway station and the Minnewater Park. The rooms are as cheap as they come, but are clean and comfortable. Each has a sink; shared toilets and shower rooms are on the landing.

Montanus

Nieuwe Gentweg 78; tel: 050 33 11 76; www.montanus.be; bus: 1, 11; €€€€

This historic house was once the home of a Belgian statesmen; now it is the picture of restrained elegance, with rooms in muted natural tones either in the mansion or in the colonial-style pavilion in the garden, a 1920s former boarding school, where there is also a cedarwood honeymoon suite. Of the 20 rooms, one is suitable for disabled guests.

The Pand

Pandreitje 16; tel: 050 34 06 66; www.pandhotel.com; bus: 6, 16; €€€

This award-winning 23-room hotel is located near the prettiest view in Bruges centre, the famous Rozenhoedkaai. Formerly an 18th-century carriage house, it is now a boutique hotel brimming with style. Bedrooms are appealing, if on the small side. The breakfast room is fur-

Four poster at The Pand

nished in country-house-kitchen style and breakfasts are famously good.

Die Swaene
Steenhouwersdijk 1; tel: 050 34 27 98; www.dieswaene.com; bus: 6, 16; €€€€
It's hard not to fall in love with this lovely hotel along a quiet, tree-lined canal close to the centre. It is in an irresistible building, with old wooden staircases and heavy oak furniture. The 22 rooms come in different sizes and styles, some of them replete with elegant four-poster beds, some – the downstairs rooms – on the dark and poky side. A candle-lit restaurant, pool and sauna add to the allure and charm of the place. The hotel-owned Pergola Kaffee across the canal also has an enviable location.

De Tuilerieen
Dijver 7; tel: 050 34 36 91; www.hotel tuilerieen.com; bus: 0/Centrum; €€€€
The most luxurious hotel in town: a 45-room pale pink mansion facing the main canal. With courteous staff and a series of plush, antique-stuffed rooms, this is a hotel that is hard to resist returning to. Some rooms have views of the canal, while others face the garden; size can vary quite a bit, though, so check what you're getting. There is also a bright swimming pool and hammam.

West
Dukes' Palace
Prinsenhof 8; tel: 050 44 78 88; www.hotel dukespalace.com; bus: 0/Centrum; €€€€

An exclusive choice occupying the neo-Gothic Prinsenhof, a 19th-century rebuild of the medieval Princes' Court created by Burgundian Duke Philip the Good in 1429. Following a major renovation in 2008, it now boasts 21st-century standards of luxury (pool, banqueting facilities, car park) and bags of historic cachet.

Ensor
Speelmansrei 10; tel: 050 34 25 89; www.ensorhotel.be; bus: 0/Centrum; €
This friendly 12-room hotel occupies a brick building on a quiet canal close to 't Zand. The rooms are plainly furnished but well-maintained, and some are quite large, with enough beds for up to four people. All have en-suite facilities with shower and WC, making this one of the best budget hotels in the city. If you have a vehicle, you can reserve a space in the private garage, but must do so in advance.

Karel De Stoute
Moerstraat 23; tel: 050 34 33 17; www.hotelkareldestoute.be; bus: 0/Centrum, 12; €
Named after the 15th-century duke of Burgundy Charles the Bold, this intimate hotel occupies a building that once formed part of the Prinsenhof ducal residence, where Charles held his wedding feast. Run by a friendly couple, this nine-room establishment offers a relaxed atmosphere in the heart of the Old Town. The rooms vary but are mainly spacious and attractive. Some have

A suite at Die Swaene

oak beams, while two have bathrooms located in a 15th-century circular staircase tower. There is an attractive cellar bar with a vaulted ceiling, and internet access is free. If you want to avoid steep stairs, ask for a lower floor.

Prinsenhof

Ontvangersstraat 9; tel: 050 34 26 90; www.prinsenhof.be; bus: 0/Centrum; €€€

Not to be confused with the Dukes' Palace in the former Prinsenhof, this elegant hotel is traditionally furnished, with wood panelling, chandeliers and other antiques; it has comfortable beds and excellent bathrooms. There is a warm atmosphere, and the staff will go out of their way to ensure your stay is memorable. The 16 rooms are often reserved well in advance, so book early.

Snuffel Sleep-In

Ezelstraat 47–49; tel: 050 33 31 33; www.snuffel.be; bus: 3, 13; €

A simple youth hostel with pine bunks in rooms sleeping four to 12 people (the small rooms can also be booked as private rooms for two people – in which case go for the en-suite option). Located in a traditional gabled house, it has a ground-floor bar with English newspapers, internet access, its own beer and live gigs every first and third Saturday of the month, except July and August. Beer and breakfast are cheap, and the atmosphere is perfect for young people.

North

Aragon

Naaldenstraat 22; tel: 050 33 35 33; www.aragon.be; bus: 0/Centrum; €

This well-run hotel is located in the heart of the old merchant's quarter, opposite a palace once owned by the Italian Medici family. The 42 rooms and 8 flats have been renovated in a comfortable English country-house style.

Asiris

Lange Raamstraat 9; tel: 050 34 17 24; www.hotelasiris.be; bus: 4, 14; €

A small, family-run hotel in a quiet quarter close to St Giles' Church (Sint-Gilliskerk). The 13 bedrooms are furnished in a plain, modern style aimed at families and travellers on a budget. Breakfast is included in the price, making this one of the best inexpensive hotels in town. Special rates are offered out of season.

Ter Brughe

Oost-Gistelhof 2; tel: 050 34 03 24; www.hotelterbrughe.com; bus: 4, 14; €€

This attractive hotel in the elegant St Giles quarter, 5 minutes from the centre of Bruges, has wood panelling and traditional charm, along with comfy beds. Breakfast is served in the 14th-century beamed and vaulted cellar, which was once a warehouse for goods brought along the canal. The 46 rooms are comfortable, if with a rather faded decor. Pay extra for a canal view: it's worth it.

Courtyard at The Pand boutique hotel

Bryghia

Oosterlingenplein 4; tel: 050 33 80 59;
www.bryghiahotel.be; bus: 4, 14; €€

This family-run hotel is situated in one of Bruges's most peaceful neighbourhoods, rarely visited by tourists but still very central. The 18-room hotel is in a 15th-century building once owned by Hanseatic merchants. The interior is cosy and tastefully furnished, with comfortable sofas and exposed wood beams, offering good value for the price. Some rooms enjoy a view of a sleepy canal.

Cavalier

Kuipersstraat 25; tel: 050 33 02 07;
www.hotelcavalier.be; bus: 0/Centrum; €

In spite of its slightly ramshackle external appearance, this small hotel is friendly and ordered and provides good value for the cheaper range of hotels; it is also very central. The eight rooms are larger than average for Bruges and the breakfast is better than you might expect from the class of hotel. The stairs are steep, though, so if you have heavy luggage ask for a lower room.

Ter Duinen

Langerei 52; tel: 050 33 04 37; www.hotel terduinen.eu; bus: 4, 14; €€€

A little out of the centre – read, nicely away from the crowds – 'The Dunes' takes its name from the former abbey across the canal. The owners have a stylish aesthetic and pay great attention to detail: the conservatory and formal garden are beautiful, and the rooms neutrally decorated and pleasant, many with laminate flooring. The cobbled Langerei can be busy in the day, but is quiet at night and windows are super-insulated. Air-conditioning in all rooms is a definite plus in warm weather, as it gets around the mosquitoes-versus-stuffiness dilemma that plagues many canalside properties.

Relais Oud-Huis Amsterdam

Genthof 4a; tel: 050 34 18 10;
www.martins-hotels.com; bus: 4, 14; €€€

Overlooking a canal in the heart of the old Merchants' Quarter, this romantic 44-room hotel, set in a 17th-century trading house, has a wooden staircase, beams and stunning antique furniture. There is also a pretty interior courtyard. Skip the hotel breakfast, which costs extra, and walk 5 minutes to Het Dagelijks Brood (Philipstockstraat 21) to enjoy coffee and croissants in a typical French farmhouse interior.

East

Adornes

St Annarei 26; tel: 050 34 13 36;
www.adornes.be; bus: 4, 14; €€

This pretty 20-room hotel occupies a row of traditional brick houses facing a canal in the charming St Anna quarter. The rooms are comfortable and bright, some with oak beams; decor is traditional verging on the dated. Breakfast is included in the price of the room and there are free bikes for guests' use,

Pretty hotel sign

as well as a limited number of under-ground parking spaces. Closed January.

Bauhaus

Langestraat 135–137; tel: 050 34 10 93; www.bauhaus.be; bus: 6, 16; €

Large budget hotel and youth hostel offering a variety of cheap accommodation: en- suite rooms with shower and toilet, well-appointed flats for 2–12 people, and dorms with up to eight beds. There is bike rental, a cybercafé and a bar, which, given the meagre nightlife offerings in Bruges, is lively and sociable.

Rosenburg

Coupure 30; tel: 050 34 01 94; www.rosenburg.be; bus: 6, 16; €€

A quiet hotel situated on the banks of a canal approximately a 10-min walk from the centre of Bruges. The atmosphere in this modern brick building is relaxed and friendly, staff are particularly helpful, and there are good business facilities. The 27 rooms are larger than average for the city.

Ter Reien

Langestraat 1; tel: 050 34 91 00; www.hotel terreien.be; bus: 6, 16; €€

'The Canals' hotel is an inexpensive option on the junction of two lovely canals, and occupies the house where the Symbolist painter Fernand Khnopff spent his childhood. All 26 rooms are non-smoking and are bright and comfortable, although some have rather-too-tiny bathrooms. They face the canal, courtyard or street, and prices reflect this. Breakfast can be taken in the pretty courtyard.

Bruges outskirts

Leonardo

Chartreuseweg 20; tel: 050 40 21 40; www.leonardo-hotels.com; bus: 7, 74; €€

This out-of-town option between the motorway and the centre has had a stylish makeover and offers modern amenities, including an outdoor pool with children's play area and easy parking, making it ideal for families. Most people will not want to stay this far from the centre, but a hired bike to cover the 5km (3 miles) from here to town is a good alternative to driving, a (pricey) taxi or the local bus – remember, Flanders is dead flat and all roads have good bike paths.

Ghent

Chambre Plus

Hoogpoort 31; tel: 09 225 37 75; www.chambreplus.be; tram 1 (Sint-Niklaasstraat); €€

Homeowner Mia Ackaert has created three sublime Bed and Breakfast rooms in the rear of her family's 18th-century man-sion. Ask for the Sultan Room for a wildly romantic decor inspired by the Middle East, or pick the Congo Room for jungle-print fabrics. The best (and priciest) choice is the Côté Sud, a separate apartment decorated in Mediterranean style, with a lounge, an open fire and a Jacuzzi

Bed-and-breakfasts are a cheap option

where you can take a bath under the night sky. A delicious break-fast is included in the price.

Ghent River Hotel

Waaistraat 5; tel: 09 266 10 10; www.ghent-river-hotel.be; tram 1 (Gravensteen); €€€€

This waterfront hotel near the Vrijdagmarkt evokes the trading history of Ghent. Some rooms occupy a restored 19th-century sugar factory, while others are in a 16th-century town house; the square was the site of a yarn market in the Middle Ages and the 19th century. When booking, ask for one of the rooms in the former factory, as these have oak beams, brick walls and odd industrial implements used for decoration. The rooms in the modern extension are plainer. The hotel has a rooftop breakfast room with striking views of the old city, a jetty and a fitness room.

Gravensteen

Jan Breydelstraat 35; tel: 09 225 11 50; www.gravensteen.be; tram 1 (Gravensteen); €€€€

This 19th-century mansion, once the home of an industrial magnate, has been turned into one of the city's most elegant hotels. It is situated across the water from Gravensteen Castle, of which rooms at the front have a fine view, and it has been tastefully renovated and extended. Fitness room and sauna. Disabled access. 49 rooms.

Marriott Ghent Hotel

Koreniei 10; tel: 09 233 93 93; www.marriott.com; tram 1 (Korenmarkt); €€€

An enviable location near all the sights and the upmarket chain's high standards have firmly established this newcomer. Part of the hotel fronts on Korenlei, facing the lovely Graslei and looking down to St Nicholas Bridge. Rooms are very comfortable though few have canal views. There is parking beneath the hotel.

De Haan

Auberge des Rois

Zeedijk 1; tel: 059 23 30 18; www.beach hotel.be; coast tram (De Haan aan Zee); €€

Fine modern hotel on the beach, built in De Haan's *belle époque*-villa style.

Grand Hôtel Belle Vue

Koninklijk Plein 5; tel: 059 23 34 39; www.hotelbellevue.be; coast tram (De Haan aan Zee); €€

A more traditional old villa, this superb and rather fanciful-looking domed hotel is close to the stop for the Coast Tram.

Ostend

Hotel du Parc

Marie-Joseplein 3; tel: 059 70 16 80; www.hotelduparc.be; bus: 5 from station to Marie-Joséplein; €€

A rare surviving pre-war building in Ostend, this Art Deco hotel behind the casino and the promenade has a wealth of stylish, original fittings in the bar-brasserie on the street. Get a room at the front; those at the rear can be pokey.

Erasmus hotel and restaurant

RESTAURANTS

Bruges has a long tradition of fine feasting and banqueting, a reputation its 21st-century inhabitants uphold in style. The West Flemish appreciate fresh seafood, grilled meats and the produce of the fertile interior: asparagus, endives, mushrooms and pungent Ardennes cheeses. But good food does not come cheap in a city centre thronging with tourists: avoid eating on the Markt square; consider eating a main meal at lunchtime when the best offers are available; and check the recommendations below – and in the 'Food and Drink' listings in each route chapter – for where to find a tasty meal at a fair price. Lunchtime is generally noon–2pm and dinner 7–9pm: the city shuts down early and few places are open late. Finally, it is wise to book ahead for an evening meal, even in the low season, as popular places are often booked out.

Centre

Breydel – De Coninck

Breidelsstraat 24; tel: 050 33 97 46;

> Price guide for a two-course meal for one, with glass of house wine:
> €€€€ = over 100 euros
> €€€ = 60–100 euros
> €€ = 30–60 euros
> € = below 30 euros

www.restaurant-breydel.be; Thur–Tue noon–2pm, 6–10pm; €€

Unremarkable from the outside, but those in the know will tell you that this unpretentious dining room – named after the city's famed freedom fighters and a family business for over 50 years – is the go-to address for mussels (when in season; expect a large portion), lobster and eels. Street-view tables make it possible to while away an afternoon watching tourists being trotted around in carriages.

Chez Olivier

Meestraat 9; tel: 050 33 36 59; www.chez olivier.be; Mon–Wed, Fri noon–1.30pm, 7–9.30pm, Sat 7–9.30pm; €€€

This impeccable all-white dining room overlooks the most romantic stretch of canal in Bruges, from the corner of the Meebrug. It's a peaceful and upmarket choice, with only 10 tables and set in a beautiful 16th-century building. The cuisine is refined French-Belgian, with a focus on meat. Request a table overlooking the canal.

Duc de Bourgogne

Huidenvettersplein 12; tel: 050 33 20 38; www.ducdebourgogne.be; Tue 7–9.30pm, Wed–Sun noon–2.30pm, 7–9.30pm; €€€

On a touristy street, this hotel restaurant offers old-school dining, with French-style dishes in beautiful surroundings

Dining in style at Erasmus   *The ambience is set at De Stove*

and a view over the most photographed canal scene in town. Sup like a lord on lobster and roast meat in rich sauce among the artworks and tapestries. The fixed-price menus are good value, especially for lunch.

Erasmus

Wollestraat 35; tel: 050 33 57 81; www.brasserieerasmus.com; noon–3pm, 6–10pm, closed Mon and Thur; €€
This sleek, grey-hued restaurant in the eponymous hotel is a tippler's dream, with a wide choice of beers to accompany the beer-inspired dishes: try crown of lamb with parsley and mustard, served with potato and bacon gratin made with Bush blond beer. A fair bit cheaper than nearby beer-focused eatery Den Dyver, but a bit less adventurous too. The menu changes monthly.

't Huidevettershuis

Huidenvettersplein 10–11; tel: 050 33 95 06; www.huidevettershuis.be; Mon, Wed–Fri 12–2pm, 6–10pm, Sat–Sun noon–10pm; €€
An elegant canal-side eatery (with an entrance on a handsome little square) specialising in Flemish cuisine. The building, which was formerly the Tanners' Guildhouse, dates from 1630.

Kwizien Divien

Hallestraat 4; tel: 050 33 80 27; www.kwiziendivien.be; daily noon– 2.30pm, 6.30–9.30pm; €€€
Rather tucked away down a side street beside the Hallen, this hotel restaurant

takes the back to basics approach on an adventurous journey: seabass, tuna and pork cheeks given an Italian twist, or from the Flemish selection shrimp crouquettes and beef and brown rabbit with prunes. There are tables on the suntrap courtyard to the rear, where the only noise interruptions will be the clanging bells from the Belfry next door.

Lucifernum

Twijnstraat 6–8; tel: 0476 35 06 51; www.lucifernum.be; Sun 6pm–10pm; €
Unique venue open just Sunday evening for drinks and dinner. In the private house of showman Willy Retsin, his Peruvian wife prepares paella. Gypsy musicians play occasionally amongst the hundreds of strange paintings and sculptures that deck out this former Masonic lodge.

Het Mozarthuys

Huidenvettersplein 1; tel: 050 33 45 30; Mon–Thur, Sun 10am–10pm, Fri–Sat 10am–11pm; €
Guess which famous composer's music wafts among the tables at this old-style Flemish restaurant? Yes, you can hum along to Wolfgang Amadeus while you enjoy its speciality grilled meat dishes and mussels. Lovely outdoor terrace.

Au Petit Grand

Philipstockstraat 18; tel: 050 34 86 71; www.aupetitgrand.be; Tue–Sun 6pm– midnight; €€
Fuel up on T-bone steak or rack of lamb at this pretty and popular address near

A three–Michelin–star starter at Hertog Jan

the Burg, where the speciality is fish and meat cooked on the grill, a Flemish favourite. It is compact and the locals like it here: if you're hoping for an intimate tête-à-tête, be aware that it can get crowded and so may not be the place for you. Advance reservation is advised.

Riva del Sole

Wollestraat 22; tel: 050 34 33 30; www.rivadelsole.be; Thur–Mon noon–2.30pm, 6–10.30pm; €€

Follow the Italian students from the College of Europe to the place they say does the best pizza in town, and this is where they will take you. The interior decor fulfils all the trattoria clichés – fake climbing vines and bunches of grapes – but you are not here for the setting. The menu makes some concessions to Belgian tastes, but the pizza and pasta dishes are what you come for and are reasonably priced.

De Stove

Kleine Sint-Amandsstraat 4; tel: 050 33 78 35; www.restaurantdestove.be; Fri–Mon and Thur 7–9.30pm, also Sat–Sun noon–1.45pm, closed two weeks in Jan, two weeks in June; €€€

Homely and rustic De Stove specialises in Flemish cuisine with an emphasis on creative ways with salad, fish and steaks. Try scallops on black pasta with tomato tapenade; sea bream with couscous; or stuffed aubergine and basil oil. The intimate 20-seater is unfussy, and set in an old gabled house on a pedestrianised street near the Markt. Prices are at the lower end of this bracket.

De Visscherie

Vismarkt 8; tel: 050 33 02 12; www.visscherie.be; Wed–Mon noon–2pm, 7–10pm; €€€

The subtle flavours of the sea are cooked to perfection at this top-notch fish and seafood restaurant, situated right on the Fish Market (Vismarkt). A formal establishment where the maître d' will attend to your every whim, this is ideal for a special occasion with all the frills. A few meat dishes are also available.

South

Bistro De Bekoring

Arsenaalstraat 55; tel: 050 34 41 57; Tue–Sat noon–2pm, 6.30–9.30pm; Sun noon–2pm; €€

Snug and romantic small bistro alongside the canal close to Minnewater Park, with low beams and a large old brick fireplace. Duck down and tuck in to Belgian staples such as snails in garlic butter, eels in green sauce or carbonnade flamande (beef slow-cooked in beer).

De Bron

Katelijnestraat 82; tel: 050 33 45 26; www.eethuisdebron.be; Mon–Fri 11.45am–2pm; €

A guaranteed healthy and wholesome option, this lunch-only vegetarian restaurant is spotless and bright, with an atrium at the rear. You join a table wherever there is a seat and eat the soup or dish of the day: a mixed platter that might include a

Rustic Den Dyver

Another culinary work of art at Hertog Jan

gratin, a grain and baked, steamed and raw vegetables (just choose which size dish you want; vegan option on request). You have to ring the bell to get in, but once in, the staff are friendly and helpful.

Christophe

Garenmarkt 34; tel: 050 34 48 92; www. christophe-brugge.be; Thur–Mon 6pm– 1am, closed first two weeks of August; €€€
Definitely worth leaving the beaten track (but not by too far) for an excellent dining experience at this unpretentious 'evening and night bistro'. The chef has won fans far and wide for his excellent way with no-nonsense staples, available till late into the night.

Couvert

Eekhoutstraat 17; tel: 050 33 37 87; www.couvert-brugge.be; Thur–Mon noon–2pm, 6–10pm; €€
A loving attention to its French-style cuisine, service and presentation have earned this slightly backstreet address a deservedly faithful following. The fixed-price menu is inventive and seasonal – gratin of scallops and asparagus; baked guinea fowl with stuffed mushrooms and creamy parsley sauce – while the à la carte is brief but diverse. White-dressed tables and brick-exposed walls complete the setting for an intimate, romantic experience.

Den Dyver

Dijver 5; tel: 050 33 60 69; www.dyver.be; Thur–Mon noon–2pm, 6.30–9.30pm; €€€

Embark on an adventure in taste at this family-run house renowned for inventive beer cuisine. Think guinea fowl and mint mousse in a Chimay sauce with caramel-ised figs; spicy rabbit roulade with prune and Rodenbach chutney; or classic *bouillabaisse* (fish stew) cooked with beer. All dishes come with a recommendation for accompanying Belgian beer, while desserts are prepared with genever (Belgian gin). Not cheap, but unique.

Hertog Jan

Torhoutse Steenweg 479; tel: 050 67 34 46; www.hertog-jan.com; Tue–Sat noon–1.30pm, 7–9.30pm; €€€€
This fabulous restaurant 2km (1.25 miles) south-west of Bruges has in merely seven years risen to become Belgium's third three-star Michelin restaurant. Chef Gert De Mangeleer and sommelier Joachim Boudens epitomise the new generation of Flemish cuisine, with highly creative dishes deserving of being exhibited in one of Bruges' art galleries, such is the attention to aesthetic detail. Yet many of the ingredients used come from the owners' nearby farm, while the service is warm and attentive. There is a choice of set menu and à la carte.

't Huidevettershuis

Huidenvettersplein 10–11; tel: 050 33 95 06; www. huidevettershuis.be; Mon, Wed–Fri noon–2pm, 6–10pm, Sat–Sun noon–10pm; €€
An elegant canalside eatery (with an entrance on a handsome little square)

Cockles from the Fish Market

specialising in Flemish cuisine. The building, which was formerly the Tanners' Guildhouse, dates from 1630.

Maximiliaan Van Oostenrijk

Wijngaardplein 17; tel: 050 33 47 23; www.maximiliaanvanoostenrijk.be; daily 10am–10pm; 15 Mar–15 Nov closed Wed; €€

Despite having as touristy a location as you can find in Bruges, adjacent to the Begijnhof and the Minnewater, Maximiliaan's achieves the creditable feat of not being entirely overpowered, but then it does have a lot of tables. Specialities include the traditional local stew, *waterzooï*, grilled meats and seafood.

't Pandreitje

Pandreitje 6; tel: 050 33 11 90; www.pandreitje.be; Mon, Tue, Fri, Sat noon–1.30pm, 7–9pm; €€€

Elegant and refined Franco-Belgian cuisine is served in spacious comfort in this Renaissanceera patrician house near the Rozenhoedkaai. Chef Guy Van Neste runs the kitchen and wine cellar, while his English-born wife welcomes guests. The atmosphere is formal, in a manner befitting the gastronomic dishes, which may include baked sea bass on a creamy watercress sauce with artichokes, or roasted sweetbreads with baby leeks and black truffles.

De Stoepa

Oostmeers 124; tel: 050 33 04 54; www.stoepa.be; Tue–Sat 11.45am–late, Sun from 1pm; €

This fusion bar-restaurant near the station is popular for its informal atmosphere and exotic cuisine, not to mention a walled back garden, which is a fantastic sun trap on fine days. When the trendy staff aren't too busy being too cool (or rude) to serve you, the menu is varied and vegetarian-friendly – wok dishes, curries, salads, and many nibbles with dips – but locals come here as much for a cheerful night out with friends as a serious tuck-in. The kitchen is open noon–2pm and 6pm–midnight.

Tanuki

Oude Gentweg 1; tel: 050 34 75 12; www.tanuki.be; Wed–Sun noon–2pm, 6.30–9.30pm, closed mid-July, school holiday in Feb and around 1 Nov; €€€

Step off Katelijnestraat and enter a calm Japanese interior where the rules of Zen harmony predominate and presentation is tip-top. Sushi, sashimi and teppanyaki are prepared at one end of the dining room in an open kitchen, while in winter the menu is boosted with the addition of warming options such as Sukiyaki and Shabushabu (two varieties of meat hotpot) and Yosenabe (chicken, seafood and vegetable casserole). Prices reflect the cost of the super-fresh fish and skilled chefs required for the perfect sushi.

De Visscherie

Vismarkt 8; tel: 050 33 02 12; www.visscherie.be; Wed–Mon noon–2pm, 7–10pm; €€€€

Classic Belgian dish of mussels and chips

The flavours of the sea are cooked to perfection in this top-notch fish restaurant, where the maître d' will attend to your every whim. Ideal for special occasions or formal dining with all the frills. A few meat dishes are also available.

De Witte Raaf

Hallestraat 4; tel: 050 33 80 27; www.restaurantdewitteraaf.be; Mon–Wed, Fri–Sat noon–2.30pm, 7–9.30pm; €€€
Tucked away in a side street beside the Hallen, the 'White Raven' takes luxurious ingredients on an adventurous journey: duck, foie gras, pigeon, partridge, horse meat and other delectables, some given an Italian twist. There are tables on the sun-trap courtyard to the rear, where the only noise interruptions will be the clanging bells from the Belfry next door.

't Zwaantje

Gentpoortvest 70; tel: 04 73 71 25 80; www.hetzwaantje.be; Fri–Tue noon–1.30pm, 6.30–9.30pm, closed Sat L; €€
Belgian-French cuisine is lovingly presented and served at this local treasure that tourists have never really discovered, partly because it is on the perimeter canal far from most attractions (off Katelijnestraat). Tiffany-style lamps, mirrors and candlelight will fulfill all your romantic fantasies while the welcome is homely and warm, a far cry from some of the tourist traps elsewhere. As well as good steaks, stew and skate, the chef has won prizes for his chocolate desserts. You have been warned…

West

Aneth

Marie van Bourgondiëlaan 1; tel: 050 31 11 89; www.aneth.be; Tue–Fri and 2nd Sun of month, noon–2pm, 7–9pm, Sat 7–9pm; €€€€
Local foodies who like their fish adore Aneth and book ahead to celebrate special occasions. Set in a roomy, detached house beside the Graaf Visartpark outside the ring road to the west, this place is well off the tourist circuit, but you will not regret the trip if you fancy a gastronomic preparation of the day's catch. The chef's speciality is the use of herbs preserved in alcohol, as well as other weird and wonderful accompaniments. True artistry on a plate.

Bhavani

Simon Stevinplein 5; tel: 050 33 90 25; www.bhavani.be; daily noon–2.30pm, 6–10.30pm; €€
Quality and authentic Indian cuisine – including vegetarian – served in stylish surroundings. Madras and tandoori dishes are specialties. The set lunch on weekdays is good value.

Bodega Lorena's

Loppemstraat 13; tel: 050 34 88 17; Tue–Sat noon–2.30pm, 6–9pm; €€
Spanish restaurant (not a bar) on a tiny alley off Simon Stevinplein. You can tuck in to authentic Iberian cuisine – a large selection of tapas, plus paella – in a dining room unchanged since the 1970s.

A typical Belgian salad with crevettes grises

Brasserie Forestière

Academiestraat 15; tel: 050 34 20 02; www.brasserieforestiere.be; Mon, Tue, Thur 11.30am–6pm, Fri–Sat 11.30am–2.30pm, 6–10pm; €

Reasonably priced, laid-back restaurant in an elegant town house with marble fireplaces and bare wooden tables, recently expanded into the property next door. Light meals – pasta, quiche, salads, including vegetarian options – are served by friendly, young staff.

Chagall

Sint-Amandsstraat 40; tel: 050 33 61 12; Thur–Tue 11am–11pm; €

Whether you are out for a few drinks or for a heart-warming pot of mussels in cream sauce, you may have to fight for a table on this popular bistro's terrace, which is perfect for people-watching and afternoon sun on the pedestrianised Sint-Amandsstraat. Classical music plays in the cosy interior, which has an open hearth, wooden beams and stained-glass windows. Very good value for good quality in a central location.

De Florentijnen

Academiestraat 1; tel: 050 67 75 33; www.deflorentijnen.be; Tue–Sat noon–2pm, 7–10pm; €€€

This sleek and stylish modern eatery takes its inspiration from the earlier use of the building by Florentine merchants. It has a lively buzz and dishes up classy Italian-French food, with painstaking attention to presentation.

Grand Café De Passage

Dweersstraat 26; tel: 050 34 02 32; www.passagebruges.com; daily bar 5pm–midnight and later, kitchen 6–10pm, closed Sun; €

A surprisingly good cheap-eat in an overpriced town: this long brown café in *belle époque* style is packed with tables. Locals love it and, thanks to the hostel upstairs (rather less well reputed than the café), a lively atmosphere is guaranteed. Good for ribs and grilled food, served with jacket potatoes or chips.

Guillaume

Korte Lane 20; tel: 050 34 46 05; www.guillaume2000.be; Wed–Sun D only; €€€

A traditional whitewashed cottage on a terraced street north of 't Zand houses a high-quality bistro run by owner-chef Wim Vansteelant, famous for its 'after party' once the plates are cleared. The menu includes a small but tasty selection of starters and main courses with a distinct Franco-Belgian flavour, such as mackerel stuffed with Liège potatoes and mustard ham.

De Hobbit

Kemelstraat 8; tel: 050 33 55 20; www.hobbitgrill.be; daily 6–11pm; €€

Popular and reasonably priced ribs and grilled food restaurant – 'Middle Earth cuisine', they claim – across the street from renowned beer joint 't Brugs Beertje (see page 117). The decor is dark and rustic, with low ceilings and antique kitchen implements.

Old-school Duc de Bourgogne   *Game features on many menus*

De Koetse

Oude Burg 31; tel: 050 33 76 80;
www.dekoetse-brugge.be; Fri–Wed
noon–2.30pm, 6–10pm; €€

This inviting restaurant has a rustic
Flemish interior with a blazing fire in
winter. It serves robust Flemish cooking,
including North Sea fish dishes, spare
ribs and excellent frites.

De Mangerie

Oude Burg 20; tel: 050 33 93 36; www.
mangerie.com; Tue–Sat noon–9pm; €€€

The couple who run this restaurant have
gained a reputation for the quality and
presentation of their dishes. Choose a
starter and main course from each of
four styles: modern Belgian, Mediterranean, Eastern and vegetarian; try their
scallops with creamed aubergines, confit
tomatoes and basil, or veal sweetbreads
with asparagus and vintage sherry.

De Zen

Beenhouwersstraat 117; tel: 050 33 67 02;
Mon–Fri noon– 2pm; €

A wholesome and varied dish-of-the-
day is all that is on the menu besides
soup in this vegan-friendly lunch restaurant. Its forté is macrobiotic cuisine, so
expect soya and seaweed aplenty.

North

Brasserie Souffleur

Vlamingstraat 58; tel: 050 34 82 92; www.
souffleur.be; Fri–Wed 11.30am–11pm; €€

This brisk and smart brasserie is
renowned for copious and original salads, but also meat and fish dishes,
including good mussels and chips. There
is a warming open hearth in winter and
a sunny terrace in summer. Popular with
ladies who lunch and other locals; there
is usually ample space at lunchtime, but
booking is advised in the evening.

Kok au Vin

Ezelstraat 21; tel: 050 33 95 21; www.kok-
au-vin.be; Tue–Sat noon–2pm, 6.30–
9.45pm; €€

This friendly restaurant serves up excellent Belgian fare in a chic setting. Yet
for all of its traditional dishes and warm
décor, the food is deceptively sophis-
ticated. North sea fish, local veal and
steak tartare all impress, but the eponymous coq-au-vin steals the show.

Pietje Pek

Sint-Jakobsstraat 13; tel: 050 34 78
74; www.pietjepek.com; Thur–Tue from
5.30pm; €€

Behind its art nouveau facade, this traditional (and unashamedly tourist-focused)
restaurant serves up big portions of its
speciality cheese and meat fondues, as
well as a few hearty Belgian classics.

Tom's Diner

West Gistelhof 23; tel: 050 33 33 82;
www.tomsdiner.be; Tue–Sat 6pm–1am; €€

This place is highly popular with locals,
and has exposed brick walls, candle-
lit setting and a late kitchen, serving a
successful blend of international influences.

Zeno courtyard

Trium Trattoria

Academiestraat 23; tel: 050 33 30 60; www.trattoriatrium.be; Tue–Sun 9am–9pm; €

Authentic Italian deli, take-out and eaterie in the old merchants' quarter where their compatriots once came to trade; this is the real thing, with home-made pasta and all the best produce from Italy. The deli counter and shop side sells wines, pasta, cheeses and hams.

Zeno

Vlamingstraat 53; tel: 050 68 09 93; www.restaurantzeno.be; Tue–Fri noon–2pm, 7–9pm, Sat 7–9pm; €€

Named after an alchemist in a Marguerite Yourcenar novel, this restaurant is run by a young couple who are passionate about sourcing the best ingredients and combining them in a magical way. Their one-monthly menu is composed of eight courses from which you select four to seven dishes, or else a faster lunch option. The Franco-Belgian cuisine is excellent, but if you loathe nouvelle cuisine this place is not for you.

East

Bistro Refter

Molenmeers 2; tel: 050 44 49 00; www.bistrorefter.com; Tue–Sat L and D; €€

A new venture of Geert Van Hecke (see De Karmeliet), this upmarket brasserie (refter, refectory) opened in 2009 and brings his culinary magic within the reach of mere mortals, while sparing them the pomp and ceremony of his landmark restaurant. Dishes are variations on the bistro standards: asparagus served every which way; snails, fish soup, scallops, and so on. The wine list is good and seating comfortable if not spacious. Reserve well in advance.

Ganzespel

Ganzenstraat 37; tel: 050 33 12 33; Fri–Sun 6–10pm; €

Small ancient house on a residential street with a bed and breakfast upstairs and homely feel downstairs, very reasonably priced daily menu comprises soup, salad, main course and beer, a choice of which will be explained by welcoming owner Nicky. Recommended for those on a tight budget.

In 't Nieuw Museum

Hooistraat 42; tel: 050 33 12 80; Thur–Tue 6–11.30pm, also Sun noon–3pm; €€

A simple front room in a humble terraced house, decorated like an old brown café festooned with dried hops and with a roaring open fire. It serves home-cooked Belgian favourites including eels in green sauce, grilled prawns and mussels, grilled meats, and simple oven-baked dishes such as lasagne, for no-frills dining with a warm-heart. Good beer selection.

De Karmeliet

Langestraat 19; tel: 050 33 82 59; www.de karmeliet.be; Tue–Sat noon–3pm, 6–11pm, plus Easter and Whit Sunday; €€€€

A legend beyond Belgium's borders, De Karmeliet occupies a gastronomic class

Colourful dessert at Zeno

Bistro Refter

of its own, created by indefatigable owner-chef Geert Van Hecke. Defending the three Michelin stars he's held for 12 years, he draws on Belgian specialities – North Sea fish, hop shoots, endive and asparagus. The patrician mansion has a comfortable lounge and formal dining rooms, but service can be a little stiff. Count around €150 a head depending on menu and wine choice.

Koto

Potterierei 15; tel: 050 44 31 31; www.hoteldemedici.com; Tue–Sun 7–10pm, Sun also noon– 2pm; €€€

Japanese food in stylish surroundings, in the Hotel Medici. Meat is tender and savoury, vegetables have just the right degree of crunchiness, sushi and sashimi seafood is fresh and bright, and the sake is warm. Teppanyaki grilled meat and fish are the speciality.

De Nisse

Hooistraat 12; tel: 050 34 86 51; www.denisse-brugge.be; Wed–Sat 6–10pm, Sun noon–3pm; €€

Homely fondue specialist that also has a varied beer selection. Good hearty soups, garlicky prawns and seasonal specialities. Although slightly out of the way and doing little to publicise itself, it has established a faithful following.

Rock Fort

Langestraat 15; tel: 050 33 41 13; www.rock-fort.be; Mon–Fri noon–2pm, 6.30–11pm; €€

Langestraat has become something of a gastro mecca in recent years, with new planets orbiting De Karmeliet's star. It has gained a name for fantastic food in a stylish but unstuffy setting. The chef has a strong background in French cuisine and injects other world influences to thrilling effect, such as noodle soup with gambas, pig cheeks in Arrabiata sauce, or veal haunch in a whisky sauce. It's not a large space, so be sure to book in advance.

Sans Cravate

Langestraat 159; tel: 050 67 83 10; www.sanscravate.be; Tue–Fri noon–2pm, 7–9pm, Sat 7–9pm; €€€

The self-styled 'cooking theatre', due to the open kitchen in the middle of the room, does original and super-stylish food in a decor to match. The characterful owner divides opinion between those who love him and those who hate him, but his culinary pedigree is unquestionable and the food – spit roasts a speciality – is guaranteed to win over all your senses.

Damme

De Damse Poort

Kerkstraat 29; tel: 050 35 32 75; www.damse poort.be; Thur–Tue 10am–10pm; €€

A smart old farmhouse with an elegant dining room and large back garden. Serves a variety of Flemish staples with a seafood bent – eels, oysters, prawns and sole – and teas are offered between meals.

A rustic partridge dish

De Drie Zilveren Kannen

Marktplein 9; tel: 050 35 56 77; Tue–Sun
11.30am–3pm, 5.30–11pm; €€
Seasonal French-inspired cuisine is
served up in this luxuriously decorated
restaurant, with various menu options
as well as à la carte.

De Lieve

Jacob Van Maerlantstraat 10; tel: 050 35 66
30; www.delieve.com; Wed–Sun for lunch
and dinner, Mon and Tue lunch only; €€€
In this highly regarded gourmet restaurant, owner-chef Frank Verstraete draws
on the best of French and Belgian influences, with a forte for fresh fish and a
clever way with herbs.

Ostend

Beluga

Kemmelbergstraat 33; tel: 059 51 15 88;
www.belugaoostende.be; daily noon–3pm,
6–10pm; €€
Facing the promenade (despite its
address), this restaurant is decorated in
a hip marine style. It serves everything
from warming onion soup to Belgian cav-
iar, specialising particularly in Belgian
produce. The service is friendly too.

Villa Borghese

Van Iseghemlaan 65; tel: 059 80 40 32;
Wed–Sun noon–2.30pm, 6–10.30pm; €
Cheery restaurant serving reliably tasty
Italian fare. Pizzas, pastas and a range
of Italian starters make up the lion's
share of Villa Borghese's menu. Warm
service.

Ypres

Old Tom

Grote Markt 8; tel: 057 20 15 41;
www.oldtom.be; Thur–Tue noon–2.30pm,
6–9.30pm (drinks 7.30am–11pm); €€
This hotel-bistro is favoured by the good
burghers of Ypres and serves Belgian
classics such as shrimp croquettes,
mussels and eels. Service can be slow
when the terrace gets busy.

De Ruyffelaer

Gustave de Stuersstraat 9; tel: 057 36 60
06; www.deruyffelaer.be; Fri–Sat 5.30–9pm,
Sun 11.30am–2pm, 5.30–9pm; €
Much-acclaimed restaurant, with a menu
of traditional Flemish dishes (rabbit, pork
belly, eel) following grandma's recipes
with locally sourced ingredients. The restaurant's dark wood décor, floor tiles and
open fire are reassuringly traditional.

Ghent

Avalon

Geldmunt 32; tel: 09 224 37 24; Tue–Sat
11.30am–2.30pm; €
Across the street from the Gravensteen
fortress, Avalon offers tasty organic-
vegetarian dishes such as home-made
soup served with home-baked bread, and
slices of savoury quiche. The antique-
tiled main room is a protected monument; there is also an attractive little
garden terrace.

Belfort Restaurant

Emile Braunplein 40; tel: 09 223 35 65; Tue,
Sun 11.30am–2pm, Wed–Sat 11.30am–

The ubiquitous but delicious Belgian waffles

2pm, 6–10pm; €€€
Light, bright, open-plan restaurant right in the centre of town, beneath the eaves of the new Stadshal. The open kitchen prepares posh versions of the Belgian classics.

Belga Queen

Graslei 10; tel: 09-280 01 00; Mon–Thur, Sun noon–2.30pm, 6.30–11pm, Fri–Sat noon–2.30pm, 6.30pm–midnight; €€€€
Stylish, even sexy, high-design restaurant inside a 13th-century grain storehouse, on Ghent's main section of canal. Fancy French/Belgian fare that is cheaper is you opt for the good-value midweek menus.

Brasserie HA'

Kouter 29; tel: 09 265 91 81; Mon–Sat noon–2.30pm, 6–10pm, Sun 9am–2.30pm, 6–10pm; €€€
Elegant yet cool, the Handelsbeurs Theatre's café-restaurant serves refined French and Belgian cuisine – light and breezy for lunch, candle-lit romantic for dinner. A multi-coloured modern chandelier graces the main dining room, and in the summer you can enjoy your meal seated on the lovely outside terrace overlooking the Ketelvaart canal.

Keizershof

Vrijdagmarkt 47; tel: 09 223 44 46; Tue–Sat noon–2.30pm, 6–10.30pm; €€
This large, rambling restaurant has so much space that even when it's full it won't seem crowded. Diners pile into hearty portions of Belgian and conti-

nental food, amid decor that features wooden ceiling beams, plain wood tables and fashionably tattered walls. In summer, there are outdoor tables in the courtyard.

't Klaverblad

Corduwanierstraat 61; tel: 09 225 61 17; Mon, Thur–Sat 6–10.30pm, Sun noon–10.30pm; €€
While most of the neighbouring restaurants in the Patershol try to lure you with music, 'themed cuisine' and moderate prices, 't Klaverblad is unashamedly gastronomic and expensive. French food is prepared with a Flemish twist, for serious eaters who appreciate good food.

Pakhuis

Schuurkenstraat 4; tel: 09 223 55 55; Mon–Thur noon–2.30pm, 6.30–11pm, Fri–Sat noon–2.30pm, 6.30pm–midnight; €€
Lively brasserie south of the Sint-Niklaaskerk, offering good modern Flemish and Franco-Italian cuisine. Its setting inside a restored former warehouse is especially impressive. Oyster and seafood platters are the speciality of the house.

Patiron

Sluizeken 30; tel: 09 233 45 87; Tue–Fri 11.30am–6pm, Sat 11.30am–3pm; €
A delightful bio café north of the city centre, where everything is made on the premises, including some hearty soups. The main speciality, however, is quiche, with more than 80 delicious varieties to choose from.

For a vast range of beers, try Cambrinus

NIGHTLIFE

As Bruges is a small city with no university bar the elite postgrad College of Europe, its best nightlife tends to be of the well-behaved variety: excellent classical music, contemporary dance and the odd jazz or rock gig, or quiet bars ideal for a drink among friends. If you want a thumping club, head for Ghent, Antwerp or Kortrijk: some bars have dance floors and are free, but these tend to appeal mainly to the very young. This chapter highlights the main cultural venues and a selection of bars for aperitifs or late evening drinks, including a few for dancing. It also picks some of the many festivals that Bruges puts on throughout the year, which may determine when you choose to visit.

Music, theatre and dance

Cactus Musiekcentrum

MaZ, Magdalenastraat 27, 8200 Brugge Sint-Andries; tel: 050 33 20 14; www.cactus music.be

Cactus is the city's principal rock, world and alternative concert promoter, whose main venue is the Cactus Club@MaZ (Magdalenazaal). It puts on an eclectic concert schedule featuring major international names in rock, pop, country, electronica and experimental, as well as local young bands. In early July, it holds the three-day Cactus Festival in the Minnewater Park.

Concert Hall

't Zand 34; tel: 050 47 69 99; box office: 070 22 33 02; www.concertgebouw.be

The modern Concert Hall (Concertgebouw) has been credited with helping the city prove that it is more than a living museum, buried in the past. It has a reputation for highbrow programming, with an emphasis on authentic music, performed as the composer intended. Period instrument symphony orchestra Anima Eterna, led by harpsichordist Jos van Immerseel, has been in residence since the building opened in 2002, but contemporary classical and electronica also feature. Touring ballet, modern dance and opera productions also play here. It holds an annual dance festival in December and co-produces the biennial Jazz Brugge with De Werf.

Cultuurcentrum Brugge/ City Theatre

Vlamingstraat 29; tel: 050 44 30 40; box office: 050 44 30 60; www.cultuurcentrum brugge.be

The neoclassical City Theatre (Stadsschouwburg) is the core venue of Cultuurcentrum Brugge, a network of performance spaces across the city which is anything but classical in its programming. Dance, live music (rock, pop, world and folk) and theatre form the mainstay, but visual art exhibitions also feature. Other venues include a 17th-century former chapel, the Hallen complex beneath the Belfort, and the MaZ, used by the Cactus Club.

De Werf

Werfstraat 108; tel: 050 33 05 29; www.dewerf.be

This theatre, jazz and blues venue has its own record label. Visiting artists come from all over the world, and there are monthly free jam sessions. Best known for its close association with Bruges-born jazz pianist and composer Kris Defoort, it is the motor behind the Jazz Brugge festival, which focuses on current trends in European jazz and is held biannually over one week in October (next held in 2014). Theatre productions include contemporary new works and children's and young people's theatre.

Film

Lumière

Sint-Jacobsstraat 36; tel: 050 34 34 65; www.lumiere.be

With three screens, this central venue shows arthouse and mainstream films. It is attached to the De Republiek café.

Nightlife

Barsalon

Langestraat 15; tel: 050 33 41 13; www.rock-fort.be; Mon–Fri noon–2.30pm, 5pm–1am (2am Fri); free

This trendy lounge bar-bistro occupies a sliver of a place next to Rock Fort res-

taurant; it belongs to the same team and serves smart tapas food to match. Ideal for a tête-à-tête.

B-In

Zonnekemeers Oud Sint-Jan; tel: 050 31 13 00; www.b-in.be; Tue–Sat 11am–2am; free

This designer lounge bar in the area behind Memling in Sint-Jan Museum has live DJ sets every Fri and Sat night, but can be soulless when quiet. The waterside terrace is a pleasant spot for early evening drinks, though.

't Brugs Beertje

Kemelstraat 5; tel: 050 33 96 16; www.brugsbeertje.be; Thur–Tue 4pm–midnight, Sat–Sun until 1am; free

The beer connoisseur's favourite bar in Bruges, as small inside as its reputation is large, this has become something of a mecca since it was established some 20 years ago, thanks to the knowledgeable landlord who can advise on all aspects of his 300 or so beers. Snacks and light meals are served, and there is a shop on-site where you can buy the T-shirt.

Cambrinus

Philipstockstraat 19; tel: 050 33 23 28; www.cambrinus.eu; daily 11am–11pm, later Sat–Sun; free

Under the same ownership as nearby beer store De Bier Tempel, this brasserie has similar expertise in the hallowed hop: 400 beers are on offer in a renovated pub-like decor with coloured

Packed bar

glass lamps, a long bar and table service. It also serves good portions of hearty food – including recipes cooked with beer.

Het Entrepot

Binnenweg 4; tel: 050 47 07 80; www.hetentrepot.be; Mon–Sun 9.30am–10.30pm; charge

This old customs building just outside the ring canal, north of the city, hosts everything from club nights and gigs to dance classes and jam sessions. Check website or flyers and posters around town for details of parties.

La Fuente

Vrijdagmarkt 15; tel: 0478 20 33 07; Mon, Thur, Fri, Sun 3pm–3am; Sat 10am–4am; free

An attractive bar on the west side of 't Zand square, La Fuente is run by a young couple, and popular with a slightly older crowd who just want to let loose to chart-toppers and dance-floor classics from the 70s and 80s. It's a pleasant place for either a pleasant aperitif or a late drink and a boogie.

Joey's Café

Zilversteeg 4; tel: 050 34 12 64; Mon–Sat 11.30am–2am, 3am or 4am; free

Jazzy sounds play late into the night at this small café (with an outdoor terrace) in the Zilverpand shopping centre. Run by a friendly local musician, this is a relaxed place to enjoy good music long after most of Bruges has gone to bed.

De Lokkedize

Korte Vulderstraat 33; tel: 050 33 44 50; www.lokkedize.be; Wed–Sun 6pm until late; free

A favourite, this convivial café is run by a friendly couple. The well-priced food in a candlelit setting is followed at weekends by live bands playing a variety of R&B, jazz, folk and rock. Popular with locals and often very busy, you can still show up pretty late and still get the lovely home-cooked food.

Du Phare

Sasplein 2; tel: 050 34 35 90; www.duphare.be; Wed–Mon 11.30am–midnight, Sat–Sun until later; food served: 12.30–3pm, 6pm–midnight; free

Up near the Dampoort at the end of Langerei, this music bar-brasserie has a friendly atmosphere, a varied menu (Creole, Thai, steaks) and once a month a live concert with a blues or jazz band. A large south-facing terrace beside the canal is a draw on sunny days, but after dark is its busiest time.

Retsin's Lucifernum

Twijnstraat 6–8; tel: 0476 35 06 51; Sun 6.30pm–10pm; charge

This old Bruges townhouse is only opened once a week by its owner, the eccentric artist Willy Retsin. This former Masonic lodge is packed with paintings, sculptures and curios; the bar serves rum cocktails (only), and the music is Latin American and gypsy, sometimes live.

Pageant of the Golden Tree

De Republiek

Sint-Jacobsstraat 36; tel: 050 34 02 29; www.derepubliek.be; daily 11am–late; free

A bohemian crowd comes here to discuss politics, culture and the film they have just seen at the adjacent arthouse cinema. It is also a good place to pick up flyers about parties and other events. Beware opening times are unpredictable.

Wijnbar Est

Braambergstraat 7; tel: 050 33 38 39; www.wijnbarest.be; Wed–Mon 4pm–midnight; free

A lovely shabby-chic wine bar whose female owner is passionate and knowledgeable. The daily menu of wines by the glass is chalked up on the blackboard; 90 other types are available by the bottle. Food includes platters of cheese and charcuterie, salad and pasta, all designed to enhance the tasting experience. There are intimate live concerts every Sunday from 8–10.30pm, and the music might be jazz, blues, boogie, folk or pop; entry is free.

Festivals (in date order)

Holy Blood Procession

Ascension Day; www.holyblood.com

A religious procession held every year on Ascension Day (May), in which biblical scenes are re-enacted and the relic of the Holy Blood is paraded through the city by the bishop, followed by a retinue of local people dressed as crusaders and knights. A long-established event on the Catholic Church calendar – a procession was first recorded in 1291 – you'll need to purchase tickets for seats along the route well in advance.

Cactus Festival

Early July; www.cactusfestival.be

This small-scale rock and world music festival in the Minnewater Park is adorable for its village-fete atmosphere.

Reiefeest

Third week in Aug, every five years; www.comitevoorinitiatief.be

The canal festival of theatre, pageantry, dancing and light shows is held every five years (next scheduled for 2018), involves hundreds of performers and thousands of spectators. Book a ticket to enter the central area and follow the action on the water and in the Burg.

Pageant of the Golden Tree

Late Aug, every five years; www.comitevoorinitiatief.be

Recreating a medieval festival (Praalstoet van de Gouden Boom) staged to celebrate the marriage of Charles the Bold, duke of Burgundy, and Margaret of York, this costumed pageant (next scheduled for 2017) drew 100,000 spectators in 2007.

Snow and Ice Festival

Nov–Jan; www.icesculpture.be

This ice sculpture attraction is a winter highlight: ice-artists from across northern Europe craft ice models on a designated theme.

In the Markt

A–Z

A

Admission charges

Most museums have small admissions charges (around €4–5), with reductions for children, students and people over 65. Some have free entry on a fixed day of the week or month, or on special museum open days and heritage days. Churches are normally free, although some take a charge to visit the treasury or crypt.

Age restrictions

The age of consent in Belgium is 16. The legal minimum driving age using a full licence is 18. The legal drinking age in bars is 16, or 18 for distilled and strong spirits. There is no minimum legal age for buying alcohol, except for spirits, where the legal age is 18.

B

Budgeting

Average costs in euros (€):
Glass of beer or house wine: €5–7
Main course at a restaurant: budget €13; moderate €22; expensive €30
Room for two including breakfast: cheap hotel: €80; moderate hotel: €130; deluxe hotel: €200
Single bus ticket: €1.30 in advance, €2 on the bus (zones 1 or 2)

Brugge City Card: an access-all-areas pass to the city's top sights (www.bruggecitycard.be) is €38 for 48 hours or €43 for 72 hours and includes entry to 26 museums and other paying attractions, a free canal boat tour between March and mid-November, and minimum 25 percent discounts on other things such as cultural events and bike hire. It can be purchased online, or in Bruges from the Tourist Office, hotels or city vendors.

C

Children

Bruges may be best known for its churches and museums, but there is still plenty to keep children entertained, both in the city or at the many attractions in the surrounding countryside and nearby coast. The compact size of the place and relative absence of traffic make it a much less tiring destination for kids than many city trips, and the canals and bridges add to its appeal. There are also several parks with playgrounds. Further afield are numerous attractions such as country parks and the coast, less than a quarter of an hour away by train. Young ones are also sure to enjoy the pancakes, waffles, hot chocolate and chips that are local specialities.

Entrance to city-owned museums (including the Belfry, Groeninge, Folk-

Touring the Dijver canal

lore, etc) is free for children under 13. For most other attractions, children pay a reduced price or enter for free if young.

Eating out. Taking children to restaurants is standard practice in Belgium in all except the most upmarket places. Most brasseries, cafés and lower-priced establishments have children's menus, or will adapt their dishes to suit. Children will like the *croque-monsieur* (toasted ham and cheese sandwich; with an egg on top: *croque-madame*), omelettes, plates of ham and cheese chunks that most bars serve as snacks, and the tiny North Sea shrimps, which are served stuffed in tomatoes or deep-fried in a white sauce *(garnalkroketten)*.

Hotels. Most hotels will have family rooms or be able to provide a child's bed on request. Check in advance for availability. The more upscale hotels can also arrange babysitting, if required.

The coast. The coast near Bruges has wide and safe sandy beaches, dunes, and a gentle gradient into the sea. Most resorts have child-friendly markers along the beach – bright-coloured animals on posts – so that children can easily locate the spot where their family is sitting. **De Haan** has a minigolf course and a small enclosure with goats and rabbits, and here and in other resorts there are many places that rent out pedal-powered buggies for driving along the promenade, as well as bikes. At **Ostend** there is a good museum aboard a former Icelandic trawler and a navy training ship, the *Mercator*, open

to visitors in the attractive town-centre marina. A ride on the **kusttram** (coast tram) is also fun, although parents – and, indeed, anyone – should be extra careful when crossing the coast road at any point, as the tram travels very fast down the central reservation, and accidents are not uncommon.

Climate and clothing

Weather can be changeable in Bruges, as it is just 12km (7 miles) from the North Sea coast and has a maritime climate. Light layers of clothing are most suitable in late spring to early autumn, with rainproof and warm layers for evenings. In winter, although snow is rare, icy winds sweep over the polders from the north and east, and a warm coat with hat, scarf and gloves are advisable. Belgians tend to prefer a discreet, smart-casual style, but all styles are tolerated. Above all, wear comfortable shoes suitable for walking on cobbled streets; avoid stilettos.

Crime and safety

Crime is generally not a worry in Bruges, although you cannot entirely rule it out. As in any popular tourist area, keep an eye on your belongings. If you arrive via Brussels, be particularly vigilant in Brussels Gare du Midi station, where thieves and pick-pockets are active. Bagsnatching is also common in international trains, especially between Brussels and Paris and Amsterdam. Thieves often work in teams of two or three and try to distract

Hotel signs on the Markt

victims by asking questions, spilling food or drink, or telling travellers they have spilled something on their clothes.

Customs

There are no import limitations between EU countries as long as the goods are for personal use. Over-18s can import: 800 cigarettes, 400 cigarillos, 200 cigars, 1kg tobacco; 10 litres spirits, 20 litres fortified wine, 90 litres wine (or 60 litres sparkling) and 110 litres beer.

People arriving from non-EU countries may bring a maximum of 1l spirits, 4l wine, 16l beer and 200 cigarettes or 50 cigars or 250g of tobacco, without paying value added tax or customs duties.

When shopping in Belgium, airport shops offer tax-free prices for people travelling to a non-EU country.

Anyone entering or leaving the EU will have to declare if they are carrying cash amounting to more than €10,000, or equivalent in other currencies.

D

Disabled travellers

Bruges is not particularly accessible due to its historic character; the narrow and cobbled streets can inhibit wheelchair use. Suitable accommodation should be booked well in advance. However, many museums have disabled access, while help with train travel can be arranged at stations, or contact the Tourist Office.

The Accessible Travel Info Point is an organisation set up by the Flemish Tourist Board to provide information for travellers with disabilities. See www.toegan kelijkreizen.be.

E

Electricity

Electrical voltage in Belgium is 220 volts at 50 Hz. Plugs are round two-pin types. Adaptor plugs can be purchased at the airport or in hardware stores.

Embassies and consulates

Australia: Kunstlaan 56, 1000 Brussels; tel: 02 286 05 00
Canada: Avenue de Tervuren 2, 1040 Brussels; tel: 02 741 06 11
New Zealand: Avenue des Nervien 9-31, 1000 Brussels; tel: 02 512 1040
Republic of Ireland: Chaussée d'Etterbeek 180, 1040 Brussels; tel: 02 282 34 00
South Africa: Rue Montoyer 17, 1000 Brussels; tel: 02 285 44 00
UK: Avenue d'Auderghem 10, 1040 Brussels; tel: 02 287 62 11
US: Boulevard du Régent 27, 1000 Brussels; tel: 02 811 40 00

Emergencies

Ambulance, Fire: 100
Police: 101
General emergency number: 112
You can also call the Bruges police on 050 44 88 44 or visit the station at Lodewijk Coiseaukaai 2, just outside the perimeter canal in the north of the city.

Flags fly outside the Concert Hall

Etiquette

Belgians greet each other by shaking hands or kissing on the cheek. In more formal situations or with people you do not know, shake hands. Close acquaintances will kiss each other once, or to mark a special occasion or after a long absence three times on alternate cheeks; but never twice. The exception is in Brussels, where expats have adopted the French-style two-kiss greeting. Men sometimes kiss each other if they are of the same family or long-standing close friends.

If you are invited as a guest to the home of a Belgian, take flowers or good-quality chocolates as a gift to the hostess. Wine or spirits should only be given to close friends.

Gay and lesbian visitors

Belgium is a very gay-friendly country. It was the second country in the world (after the Netherlands) to legalise same-sex marriage, in January 2003. In 2006, gay couples gained the same rights as heterosexuals to adopt children. Bruges is not known for having a large gay community and certainly has a discreet party scene, but it is a very tolerant place and most venues are gay-friendly.

The website www.j-h.be/gaybruges lists social events and the addresses of restaurants, bars and hotels where gay folk are especially welcome, as well as the contacts required to organise a gay wedding.

Green issues

Bruges has an enviable environmental situation. Refreshed by North Sea winds and encircled by grassy fields reclaimed from the sea centuries ago for farmland, it is a model of sustainable town planning, served by excellent public transport and flat enough to encourage anyone to hop on a bike. The only serious threats to the environment are to be found on the outskirts of the city and around Zeebrugge port, where development pressure has provoked fierce protest and the creation of a militant 'green belt' movement.

The city's canals have been cleaned up in recent decades; private boats are forbidden and fish have returned. The Flemish region claims to be the world champion of recycling: over 70 percent of domestic waste is separated for recycling. The public transport network is exemplary, here and throughout densely populated Belgium: buses serve the tiniest villages and the entire coastal strip is connected by an efficient tram service, which connects with trains to all cities. Generous public subsidies for renewable energy and public transport passes have also proved successful in changing public attitudes.

Carbon-offsetting

Air travel produces a huge amount of carbon dioxide and is a significant con-

Classic Bruges architecture

tributor to global warming. If you would like to offset the damage caused to the environment by your flight, a number of organisations can do this for you, using online 'carbon calculators', which tell you how much to donate. In the UK travellers can visit www.climatecare.org or www.carbonneutral.com; in the US go to www.climatefriendly.com or www.sustainabletravelinternational.org.

H

Health

Healthcare and insurance
EU Nationals who fall ill in Belgium are eligible to receive emergency treatment. You will have to pay, but are entitled to claim back 75 percent of the cost of seeing a doctor or dentist and of prescription drugs. You will have to pay part of the costs of hospital treatment. Ambulance travel is not covered.

To receive a refund you need a European Health Insurance Card. For UK citizens, these are available online at www.dh.gov.uk, by picking up an application form in a post office. Irish citizens should visit www.ehic.ie. Reimbursements are handled in Belgium by Sickness Funds Offices (Mutualité/Ziekenfonds).

Non-EU citizens are advised to take out medical insurance before travelling.

The following non-profit group also offers members fixed rates for medical treatment abroad: International Association for Medical Assistance to Travellers (IAMAT), 2162 Gordon Street, Guelph, Ontario, N1L 1G6, Canada; tel: 519 836 0102; www.iamat.org. Members receive a medical record completed by their doctor and a directory of English-speaking IAMAT doctors on call 24 hours a day. Membership is free, but donations are appreciated.

Pharmacies and hospitals
Pharmacies are identifiable by a green neon cross sign. Most are open Mon–Sat 9am–6pm. All pharmacies display in their window details of pharmacies *(apotheek)* that are on duty at night and weekends, or call 0900 10 500 (8.30–10pm).

The main Bruges hospital (including for A&E) is AZ Sint-Jan, Ruddershove 10; tel: 050 45 21 11; www.azsintjan.be.

Telemedicine
The non-profit organisation Health Care Belgium was set up in 2007 to promote Belgium as a centre of medical excellence and encourage the delivery of medical services to foreign patients in an ethical and coordinated way. See www.healthcarebelgium.com.

Hours and holidays

The standard business hours in Belgium are 8am–5pm or 9am–6pm. Shops usually open at 10am, sometimes closing for lunch. Banks close at 4pm and over the weekend. Most museums are closed on Mondays; shops are closed on Sundays and many on Mondays too,

Rosary Quay at night

although in tourist destinations such as Bruges and the coastal resorts many stay open.

I

Internet facilities

Internet cafés are not widely visible in Bruges as most residents have fast broadband at home and the city is not a major student or backpacker destination. Many hotels offer email facilities, although they may charge a high price for the service. Youth hostels offer an alternative; two are included below:
Bauhaus, Langestraat 133-137; tel: 050 34 10 93; www.bauhaus.be
Snuffel Sleep-In, Ezelstraat 47–49; tel: 050 33 31 33; www.snuffel.be

L

Language

The language of Flanders is Dutch, or, correctly, 'Netherlandic'. Belgium has three official languages: Dutch (spoken by 58 percent of the population), French (31 percent, including a majority in Brussels) and German (11 percent), although English is widely spoken. For more on this, and some useful vocabulary to help you communicate once you're in Belgium, see page 132.

Left luggage

The railway station in Bruges has lockers and a staffed facility for left luggage. Opening hours are daily 6am–9.30pm.

Lost property

For property lost on a train or in a station, see www.belgianrail.be/en/cust omer-service/lost-objects.aspx, and report your lost object online. Or call Bruges station lost property on 050 30 23 28.

If you lose your passport, contact your embassy or consulate to arrange temporary travel documents. For other lost items, contact the police, see page 122.

M

Maps

You will not normally need a map other than the one provided in this book. However, if you plan to travel outside the city by public transport, pick up a De Lijn map from the booth by the railway station or the Tourist Office on 't Zand. Detailed topographical maps of Belgium are published by the National Geographic Institute, see: www.ngi.be

Media

Print media

Media ownership is largely in Belgian hands and highly concentrated into Flemish- and French-language press. There are numerous national and local newspapers; the main Flemish ones are *De Standaard* (quality, centre right), *De Morgen* (quality, centre left) and *Het Laatste Nieuws* (tabloid). The national news agency is Belga.

Be sure to try Belgian beers

Radio

The Flemish public service broadcaster VRT (www.vrt.be) has the largest audience share in the Dutch-speaking north of Belgium. Its main stations are Radio 1 (news, talk and gameshows), Radio 2 (mainstream music), Klara (classical) and Studio Brussel (rock and alternative). The big commercial stations are Nostalgie (classic rock), Q Music (pop and rock) and Radio Contact.

Television

Over 90 percent of Belgian households have cable TV, which shows Belgian public and commercial channels as well as public television from France, the Netherlands, Germany and the UK. CNN, BBC World, MTV, Eurosport and CNBC are widely available. Digital TV has been slow to take off in Belgium due to the preponderance of cable.

English-language publications

Ackroyd Publications produces *The Bulletin*, which covers news, arts and lifestyle in Belgium, especially Brussels, and runs website www.xpats.com for the international community in Belgium.

Money

Currency

Belgium uses the euro (€), which is divided into 100 cents. There are 5, 10, 20, 50, 100, 200 and 500 euro notes, coins that are worth €1 and €2, and 1, 2, 5, 10, 20 and 50 cent coins.

Credit cards

All major cards are accepted (Visa, MasterCard, Maestro, American Express and Diners Club). Most shops, restaurants and hotels accept credit cards, but few cafés or bars do.

Cash machines

There are plenty of ATMs in the city and most take credit cards. Those that are contained within a bank's entrance porch are accessible during bank opening hours only, unless you have a Belgian Bancontact-Mister Cash card.

Traveller's cheques

Traveller's cheques are widely accepted.

Tipping

Service charges and taxes are always included in prices. However, many people round up the bill in a café or restaurant (especially if they are in a group) to show appreciation, usually between €0.5–3. Suggested tip for porter service is €1 per item, cloakroom attendants €1.25–2.50 per coat. Most public toilets require a tip to the attendants of 25–50 cents.

Taxes

Belgian VAT (21 percent, or 6 percent in certain sectors) is included in prices.

Post

The Belgian post office (De Post/La Poste) is nationalised and efficient,

A local mailbox

although thefts from packages are not uncommon. Mailboxes are red. Buy stamps from post offices and shops selling postcards. The cost of sending a regular-size postcard or letter weighing no more than 50g is €1.13 within Europe or €1.34 to other countries.

The main Bruges Post Office is on the Markt: Markt 5; tel: 022 01 23 45; www.post.be; Mon–Fri 9am–6pm, Sat 9am–3pm.

Public holidays

1 January New Year's Day
1 May Labour Day
21 July National Day
15 August Assumption
1 November All Saints' Day
11 November Armistice Day
25 December Christmas Day
Movable dates: **Easter** (varying), **Easter Monday** (1st Monday after Easter), **Ascension** (6th Thursday after Easter), **Pentecost** (7th Sunday after Easter) and **Pentecost Monday** (8th Monday after Easter). Holidays falling on a weekend are taken the following Monday.

Religion

Belgium is a strong defender of religious freedom. Most Belgians are Roman Catholic (75 percent, but just 10 percent practising), but five other religions are recognised by the state: Protestantism, Islam, Orthodox, Judaism and Anglicanism. The federal government pays wages to their ministers. Religious or 'moral' teaching is obligatory in schools; children are instructed according to their choice in any of the six recognised religions or in non-religious ethics.

Smoking

Smoking is banned in restaurants and bars, though bars may provide a separate smoking area. Smoking is forbidden on public transport, in enclosed public spaces and in most workplaces, although smoking rooms are often provided.

Student travellers

Students and young people may be entitled to reduced-rate admission to many museums, but a passport or student identity card may be required as proof of age and validity.

Telephones

Fixed-line telephone numbers in Bruges start 050. You need to use the area code. The code for Belgium is +32. When dialling from abroad, omit the first 0 of the code. For English-speaking directory enquiries, tel: 1405. For online information: www.infobel.be

Prepaid calling cards can offer a substantial saving on standard rates and can be used from a fixed phone, pay phone or mobile phone. Cards are

Bikes are great for touring

widely available, including in train stations, newspaper stands and supermarkets.

To make an international call, dial 00, followed by the country code (Australia +61, Canada +1, Ireland +353, UK +44, US +1), then the area code and number. Public telephones are very limited in Bruges.

Mobile (cell) phones

If you come from North America, you will not be able to use your phone if it is a single-band device. If you have an unlocked dual-band GSM cell phone, you can buy a prepaid SIM card locally to avoid roaming charges. The three main mobile phone operators in Belgium are Proximus, Mobistar and Base.

Time zones

Belgium is GMT+1 hour (+2 Apr–end Oct). When it is noon in Bruges, it is 11am in London, 6am in New York, 10pm in Sydney.

Toilets

Public toilets are not widely available in Bruges: there are toilets at the station and by the Minnewater in the park. Some cafés charge for using the toilet, so non-patrons are free to use them too.

Tourist information

Toerisme Brugge, the tourist information service, is helpful and efficient. Staff are fluent in English. The main tourist information bureau In&Uit is on the ground floor of the Concert Hall, 't Zand 34; tel: 050 44 46 46; www.bruges. be/toerisme; Mon–Sat 10am–5pm, Sun until 2pm. There are other offices at Historium, Markt 1 (daily 10am–5pm) and the railway station (Mon–Fri 10am–5pm, Sat–Sun until 2pm).

Outside the country, contact the Flemish or Belgian tourist office:
UK: Tourism Flanders-Brussels, Flanders House, 1a Cavendish Square, London W1G OLD; tel: 020 7307 7738; www.visit-flanders.co.uk
US: Belgian Tourist Office, 220 East 42nd Street, Suite 3402 New York, NY 10017; tel: 212 758 8130; www.visit belgium.com

Tours and guides

Bike tours

Quasimundo bike tours run Mar–Oct, 9.50am, starting at Toyo Ito pavilion on the Burg (reservation required). Knowledgeable and entertaining guides lead bike tours of the city. Children under 8 free (Nieuwe Gentweg 5; tel: 050 33 07 75; www.quasimundo.com).

Canal rides

There are several jetties for boat tours: behind the Church of our Lady (Onze-Lieve-Vrouwekerk), along the street the Dijver, beside the Fish Market (Vismarkt) and on Rozenhoedkaai. For information: Katelijnestraat 4; tel: 050 33 27 71; www.nvstael.com; Mar–Nov 10am–6pm. Boats sometimes operate out of season if the weather is good.

Ostend's boardwalk

Horse-drawn carriages

The horse-drawn carriage tours depart from the Markt (Burg on Wed) and can carry 5 adults. The tour takes 35 minutes, including a drink-stop for the horse at the Beguinage, where passengers can get off and visit. See De Brugse Koetsiers, p/a Gemene Weidestraat 51; tel: 050 34 54 01; www.hippo.be/koets; daily 9.30am–5.30pm.

Bruges–Damme by paddle-steamer

The 'Lamme Goedzak' paddle-steamer moors at Noorweegse Kaai 31, just beyond Dampoort, and departs several times a day for Damme, 7km (4 miles) away, before making the return trip. The journey takes half an hour. See Damme Tourist Office; tel: 050 28 86 10; www.bootdamme-brugge.be; 1 Apr–15 Oct; five departures daily each way.

Battlefield tours

Tour operators Quasimodo (tel: 050 37 04 70; www.quasimodo.be) and Visit Bruges (tel: 050 34 60 60; www.visit bruges.org) organise trips to Ypres from Bruges. Within Ypres, Flanders Battlefield Tours (tel: 057 36 04 60; www. ypres-fbt.com) and Over The Top Tours (tel: 057 42 43 20; www.overthetop tours.be) are just two of several local tour guides, which can tailor visits on request.

Transport

Airports and arrival

The majority of international airlines fly into Brussels airport (tel: 0900 700 00,

+32 27 53 77 53 (from abroad); www. brusselsairport.be) near Zaventem, 12km (7 miles) northeast of Brussels. A train station beneath the airport has direct services to Brussels and Ghent, from where connecting services take you to Bruges. The journey via Brussels or Ghent (both one change) takes 1 hour 30 mins. A taxi ride will cost around €175.

Low-cost airlines use Brussels South–Charleroi airport (www.charleroi-airport.com), 50km (30 miles) to the south. Coaches ferry passengers to and from Brussels in around 1 hour (see Voyages L'Elan; www.voyages-lelan.be).

Paris and Amsterdam airports are also within reach via high-speed train to Brussels, then inter-city train to Bruges.

By sea

Cross-channel ferries from the UK serve seaports in easy reach of Bruges.
Dover–Calais: Only P&O Ferries (tel: 08716 642 121; www.poferries.com) now operates on this busy route, with several ferries daily. Crossings take 90 minutes. Calais is 120km (75 miles) from Bruges.
Dover–Dunkirk: Norfolkline schedules about 11 crossings daily each way, journey time 2 hours (tel: 0871 574 7235; www.norfolkline.com). Dunkirk is 76km (47 miles) from Bruges.
Ramsgate–Ostend: Transeuropa Ferries operate eight passenger crossings daily, taking 4 hours (tel: 0844 493 0651; www.transeuropaferry.co.uk). Ostend is 30km (18 miles) from Bruges.

Hull–Zeebrugge: P&O Ferries run a nightly service from Hull to Zeebrugge (every other night in January). Journey time around 12 hours.

By rail

International trains from Paris, London and Amsterdam stop in Brussels. Eurostar services from London (St Pancras) and Kent (Ebbsfleet or Ashford) serve Brussels in under 2 hours, up to 10 times a day. Fares include free onward travel on Belgian railways to any Belgian station (within 24 hours of the arrival time stamped on the Eurostar ticket). See www.eurostar.com for reservations, or tel: 08432 186 186; outside UK, tel: +44 1233 617 575.

Trains to Bruges run around twice an hour from Brussels, and take just under 1 hour. For timetables, see the Belgian railways (SNCB/NMBS) website (www.b-rail.be). Intercity trains (IC) are comfortable, with toilets but no refreshments. They are often crowded at weekends and in the summer. The main station lies just outside the Old City. It takes about 10 minutes to walk into town; there are also frequent shuttle buses from the station to the Markt.

By road

Bruges is located near the E40 motorway. The drive from Brussels takes just over 1 hour outside of peak times. Drivers from Britain can take the Eurotunnel from Folkestone to Calais, a drive-on, drive-off train service that takes 35 mins, or 1 hour from motorway to motorway. The service runs 24 hours a day, all year, with up to five departures an hour. Book in advance for best prices and to avoid a wait. Toll booths accept cash, cheques or credit cards. The price applies to the car, regardless of the number of passengers or car size. Eurotunnel (UK tel: 08443 353 535; www.eurotunnel. com). From Calais, allow 1 hour 20 mins to drive to Bruges (follow signs to Brugge Centrum).

Public transport

Bus. As Bruges is so compact, you will rarely need to use the city buses, which are all operated by Flemish public transport company De Lijn (www.delijn. be). The central loop bus service (0/ Centrum) links the rail station, 't Zand and the Markt. A single ticket bought on the bus costs €2 (€1.30 when purchased in advance) for 1 or 2 zones and €3 (€2 in advance) for 3 or more zones, and is valid for 1 hour (including any change of bus within the Bruges zone). Day passes and 5/10-journey passes are also available and save money. Tickets must be entered in the scanner machine by the doors whenever you board a bus.

Taxis. In Bruges taxis can be recognised by the insignia on their roof. There are stands at the station and the Markt square.

Brugse Taxi: tel: 050 33 44 55; http://

17:31	KNOKKE	IC	8A	18:05	00
17:33	KORTRIJK	IC	7	18:07	KO
17:34	BLANKENBERGE	IC	8B	18:09	ZE
17:35	BRUSSEL TONGEREN	IC	5	18:13	KN
17:37	OOSTENDE	IC	6	18:25	00
17:37	GENT SINT-PIE...S	L	2	18:31	KN
17:54	OOSTENDE	P	10	18:33	KO
17:57	ANTWERPEN L	IC	8	18:34	BL
18:00	OOSTENDE	IC	10	18:35	BR

Bruges has great rail connections

brugsetaxiservice.westsite.be

Rony's Taxis: tel: 050 34 43 44; www.ronystaxis.com

Taxi Snel: tel: 050 36 36 49; www.taxisnel.be

Driving. Driving and parking within Bruges centre is not advised, as the old centre is a network of one-way streets. Tourists are advised to leave vehicles at the large car park next to the station (Stationsplein) or one of the other car parks in the city. Drop baggage at your hotel first. The charge for parking here is reasonable and includes free travel on the city buses. Claim a free ticket for each person in the car by showing your car park ticket at the De Lijn office outside the station.

Driving is on the right, with overtaking on the left. Vehicles coming from the right always have priority unless road markings indicate otherwise. Roads are generally safe, but speeding can be a problem. The blood alcohol limit for drivers is 0.5mg/litre (one glass of wine). Police have the power to carry out random alcohol tests.

Car hire. The minimum age for car hire is 21 or 22 (some firms charge higher rates to those under 25). You need a passport, driving licence (valid for at least one year) and a credit card, on which a deposit is blocked until the vehicle is returned.

Budget: tel: 02 730 62 11; www.budget.be

Hertz: tel: 02 717 32 01; www.hertz.be

Avis: tel: 070 22 30 01; www.avis.be

Visas and passports

EU nationals require only a valid personal identity card or passport to visit Belgium. Visitors from the US, Canada, Australia or New Zealand need a valid passport but not a visa if staying for less than three months.

Nationals of other countries may need a visa, costing around €60 (for a short-stay visa), which should be obtained from the embassy or consulate responsible for your place of residence before you travel. Apply 3–4 weeks prior to departure. Your passport must be valid for three months longer than the visa.

For more information (and if visiting for over 90 days), check www.diplomatie.be or with the Belgian embassy in your home country. Belgian law requires everyone over the age of 12 to carry an identity card or passport at all times.

Women

Women in Belgium have equal rights, and it is safe for women to travel alone. In cities, dress conservatively if walking around at night and be aware of bag-snatchers and pickpockets; this is more of a problem in Brussels and Antwerp than in Bruges. Unwelcome approaches are best deterred by a firm but friendly response.

Look out for the green cross when seeking a pharmacy

LANGUAGE

The people of Flanders speak Dutch. Behind this simple statement lies a thicket of complication. There is no such language – the word reflects the historical English inability to distinguish between the languages of Germany (Deutsch) and the Low Countries (Nederlands), and their lumping of them together and corrupting it to Dutch. The language academy of Flanders calls its language 'Netherlandic', but is willing to live with Dutch as an internationally accepted substitute. If this is far too complicated, most people in Bruges are happy to speak English or German (but not necessarily French).

As a rule, the 'hard consonants' such as t, k, s and p are pronounced almost the same as in English, but sometimes softer. Other pronunciations differ as follows: *j = y; v = f; je = yer; tje = ch; ee = ay; oo = o; ij = eay; a = u.*

Useful phrases

General
Yes *Ja*
No *Nee*
Please *Alstublieft*
Thank you (very much) *Dank u (wel)*
Excuse me *Excuseer/pardon*
Hello *Dag/Hallo*
Goodbye *Dag/tot ziens*
Good morning *Goedemorgen*
Good afternoon *Goedemiddag*
Good evening *Goedenavond*
Do you speak English? *Spreekt u Engels?*
I don't understand *Ik begrijp het niet*
I am sorry *Het spijt me/Sorry*
No problem *Geen probleem*
Can you help me? *Kunt u mij helpen?*
What is your name? *Wat is uw naam?/Hoe heet u?*
My name is… *Ik heet…*
I am English/American *Ik ben Engelsman/Engelse/Amerikaan*
When? *Wanneer?*
At what time? *Hoe laat?*
What time is it? *Hoe laat is het?*
today *vandaag*
yesterday/tomorrow *gisteren/morgen*
now/later *nu/later*
this morning *vanmorgen*
this afternoon *deze namiddag/vanmiddag*
this evening *vanavond*
day/week *dag/week*
month/year *maand/jaar*
here/there *hier/daar*
left/right *links/rechts*

On arrival
How do I get to… from here? *Hoe kom ik van hier naar…?*
Is there a bus to…? *Is/Gaat/Rijdt er een bus naar…?*
railway station *station*
I want a ticket to… *Ik wil graag een kaartje naar…*

Arm yourself with a few words of Dutch

single (one way) *enkele reis*
return (round-trip) *retour/heen en terug*
first/second class *eerste/tweede klas*
Do you have any vacancies? *Hebt u een kamer vrij?*
a single room *een eenpersoonskamer*
a double room *een tweepersoonskamer*
What is the charge per night? *Hoeveel is het per nacht?*
May I see the room? *Kan ik de kamer bekijken?*

Sightseeing

I am looking for... *Ik zoek…naar*
Where is...? *Waar is hier…?*
tourist information office *de toeristische dienst*
museum *het museum*
church *de kerk*
exhibition *de tentoonstelling*
When does the museum open/close? *Wanneer is het museum open/gesloten?*

Emergencies

Help/Stop! *Help/Stop!*
Call a doctor/an ambulance *Bel een dokter/een ziekenwagen*
Call the police/fire brigade *Bel de politie/brandweer*
Where is the nearest telephone/hospital? *Waar is de dichtstbijzijnde telefoon/het dichtstbijzijnde ziekenhuis?*
I do not feel well *Ik voel me niet goed/lekker*
I have lost my passport/money/handbag *Ik heb mijn paspoort/geld/handtas*

Dining out

breakfast *het ontbijt*
lunch *de lunch/het middageten*
dinner *het diner/avondeten*
meal *de maaltijd*
menu *de (spijs) kaart/het menu*
Can we see the menu? *Kunnen we de (spijs) kaart bekijken?*
first course *het voorgerecht*
main course *het hoofdgerecht*
the bill *de rekening*
I am a vegetarian *Ik ben vegetariër*
I'd like... *Ik wil/zou graag…*
What do you recommend *Wat beveelt u aan?*

Shopping

How much is it? *Hoeveel is/kost het?*
Where can I buy...? *Waar kan ik… kopen?*
Have you got...? *Hebt u…?*
Can I have...? *Mag ik … hebben?*
What size is it? *Welke maat is het?*
cheap/expensive *goedkoop/duur*
I will take it *Ik neem/koop het*
Do you take credit cards? *Aanvaardt u kredietkaarten?*
Is there a bank near here? *Is er hier een bank in de buurt?*

Days of the week

Monday *Maandag*
Tuesday *Dinsdag*
Wednesday *Woensdag*
Thursday *Donderdag*
Friday *Vrijdag*
Saturday *Zaterdag*
Sunday *Zondag*

BEGIJNENVEST

A street sign in Bruges

Numbers

0 *nul*
1 *een*
2 *twee*
3 *drie*
4 *vier*
5 *vijf*
6 *zes*
7 *zeven*
8 *acht*
9 *negen*
10 *tien*
20 *twintig*
21 *een en twintig*
30 *dertig*
40 *veertig*
50 *vijftig*
60 *zestig*
70 *zeventig*
80 *tachtig*
90 *negentig*
100 *honderd*
1,000 *duizend*

Online

Where's an internet café? *Waar vind ik een internetcafé?*
Does it have wireless internet? *Is er draadloos internet?*
What is the WiFi password? *Wat is het wifi-wachtwoord?*
Is the WiFi free? *Is wifi gratis?*
Can I…? *Kan ik…?*
print *printen*
plug in/charge my laptop/iPhone/iPad? *mijn laptop/iPhone/iPad aansluiten/opladen?*
access Skype? *Skypen?*

What's your e-mail? *Wat is uw e-mailadres?*
My e-mail is… *Mijn e-mailadres is…*

Social media

Are you on Facebook/Twitter? *Bent u op Facebook/Twitter?*
What's your user name? *Wat is uw gebruikersnaam?*
I'll add you as a friend. *Ik zal u toevoegen als vriend.*
I'll follow you on Twitter. *Ik zal u volgen op Twitter.*
I'll put the pictures on Facebook/Twitter. *Ik zal de foto's op Facebook/Twitter zetten.*

Menu reader

Appetizers

gerookte paling *smoked eel*
huzarensalade *potato, vegetables and meat with mayonnaise*
mosselen *mussels*
nieuwe haring *freshly caught, salt-cured herring*
pasteitje *pastry filled with meat or fish*
zure haring *pickled herring*

Fish

Forel *trout*
Garnaal *shrimp [prawn]*
kabeljauw *cod*
kreeft *lobster*
makreel *mackerel*
mossel *mussel*
oester *oyster*
paling *eel*

Some Dutch words aren't too dissimilar to English

sardientje *sardine*
schelvis *haddock*
school *plaice*
tonijn *tuna*
schelpdier *clam*
zalm *salmon*

Meat and poultry
biefstuk *steak*
duif *pigeon*
eend *duck*
fazant *pheasant*
kalfsvlees *veal*
kalkoen *turkey*
kip *chicken*
konijn *rabbit*
lamsvlees *lamb*
rundvlees *beef*
spek *bacon*
varkensvlees *pork*
worst *sausage*

Vegetables
aardappel *potato*
bietje *beetroot*
champignon *mushroom*
erwt *pea*
knoflook *garlic*
kool *cabbage*
kruiden *herbs*
paprika (rode/groene) *(red/green) pepper*
raap *turnip*
sla *lettuce*
sperziebonen *green beans*
ui *onion*
witlof *Belgian endive*
wortel *carrot*

zuurkool *sauerkraut*

Fruit
aardbei *strawberry*
appel *apple*
banana *banana*
druif *grape*
framboos *raspberry*
kers *cherry*
perzik *peach*
rode bes *redcurrant*
sinaasappel *orange*

Cheese
Edammer kaas *Edam mild cheese*
Friese nagelkaas *cheese from Friesland, produced with skimmed milk and cloves*
Geitenkaas *goat's cheese*
Goudse kaas *Gouda cheese*
Komijnekaas *mild, hard cheese with cumin seeds; also called Leidse kaas*
Leerdammer kaas *sweet, nutty cheese*
Maaslander kaas *Gouda-like cheese*

Dessert
appeltaart *Dutch apple tart*
chipolatapudding *pudding of eggs, biscuits and liqueur*
gebak *pastry or cake*
haagse bluf *whipped egg whites with currant sauce*
kwarktaart *light cheesecake*
pannenkoek *thin pancake*
poffertje *tiny sugared pancake*
vla *custard*
vruchtenvlaai *Limburg fruit flan*
wafel *waffle*

The Flemish poet Jacob van Maerlant

BOOKS AND FILM

Books

The city of Bruges has long provided a rich backdrop for literary works of religious inspiration, political intrigue and romance. This section introduces writers and dramatists for whom Bruges has provided creative stimulation, as well as a selection of contemporary Flemish writers who have made their mark on the Dutch-language scene.

Early writers and dramatists

Bruges had its first literary boom in medieval times. The then Cathedral of St Donatian's on the Burg had a great library, a music school and a scriptorium, where illuminated manuscripts were produced. Bookshops were clustered around the cathedral and attracted pioneers of the trade: William Caxton produced the first printed book in the English language in Bruges in 1474, a *Recuyell of the Histories of Troy*, ordered by Margaret of York, Duchess of Burgundy, before he left to introduce printing in England.

Pre-20th century

To learn more about the Bruges-inspired revolt against the French in 1302, read Hendrik Conscience's novel *De Leeuw van Vlaanderen* (The Lion of Flanders, 1838). In nearby Damme, the poet Jacob van Maerlant (1235–1300) was the greatest Flemish poet of the Middle Ages, and remained the most popular for centuries after his death. He wrote long didactic poems. Charles de Coster's *The Glorious Adventures of Tijl Uilenspiegel* (1867), inspired by a medieval character, gave the same village its legendary hero.

The Catholic priest and teacher Guido Gezelle (1830–99) was a one-man literary movement, who gave Flemish poetry a new lease of life with his volume *Kerkhofblommen* (Graveyard Flowers, 1858), a mixture of literary Dutch and the dialect of West Flanders. His ideas and beliefs brought him into conflict with the church and educational authorities, and he abandoned poetry in the 1870s in favour of writing essays and doing translations. Gezelle returned to his first love in *Tijdkrans* (Time's Garland, 1893) and *Rijmsnoer* (String of Rhymes, 1897), poems dealing with nature, religion and Flemish nationalism that show an original use of rhyme, metaphor and sound.

Georges Rodenbach (1855–98) never lived in Bruges but immortalised the city in his 1892 novel *Bruges-la-Morte*. It tells the story of a widower who has retreated to Bruges to grieve for his young wife in a city chosen for its silence, monotony and melancholy. The novel provoked a 'cult of Bruges' among Symbolist artists and

Brendan Gleeson and Colin Farrell star in 'In Bruges'

poets – Mallarmé, Rodin and Proust were fans – and inspired Thomas Mann *(Death in Venice)*, Korngold's opera *Die tote Stadt* (1920) and, it has been claimed, Hitchcock's *Vertigo*.

20th century and beyond

Pieter Aspe (b.1953) writes crime fiction best-sellers which are now in their third TV series. All based in Bruges, his stories centre on murder investigations carried out by two police officers.

Hugo Claus (1929–2008) was the most important Flemish writer of the post-World War II period. He received more awards than any other Dutch-language writer, and his work has been translated into 20 languages. His *Het verdriet van België* (1983; The Sorrow of Belgium) – an epic story of collaboration during the Nazi era – is essential reading for anyone who wants to understand modern Belgium. Claus was born in Bruges.

Bart Moeyaert (b.1964) was born and grew up in Bruges, but now lives in Antwerp. A prize-winning author, he has also had several books translated into English, including novels for young adults which deal with family problems, and *Brothers*, a collection of stories that describe his life growing up as the youngest of seven brothers (www.bartmoeyaert.com).

Peter Verhelst (b.1962), another Bruges-born writer who moved away, this time to Ghent, writes poems, novels and poetic texts for dance and the-atre productions. His poem for Brugge 2002, the city's year as European Capital of Culture, is engraved into the seatbacks of the Concertgebouw.

Paul De Wispelaere (b.1928), also born in Bruges, is a literary critic and novelist, essayist and lecturer in Dutch-language literature. Editor for years of literary journals, his works are avant-garde and examine the quest for identity and the relationship between literature and life.

Film

Martin McDonagh's Oscar-nominated black comedy *In Bruges* (2008) gave the city a starring role and put it on the map for film fans. The tower of the Belfry plays a starring role in the climactic scene of the film, set by night, and many visitors come here determined to experience the monument as seen in the film – unfortunately not possible, as it is not open to the public at night.

Other city sights that can be spotted in the film include the Minnewater Bridge, the Astrid Park, the Groeninge, the Relais Bourgondisch Cruyce Hotel (where the men are holed up; see page 97), the drinking hole t'Zwart Huis (on Kulperstraat) and the lovely restaurant Cafedraal (Zilverstraat 38; see page 33).

Other movies that feature the city include *A Nun's Story* (1959, starring Audrey Hepburn) and *Malpertuis* (1971), a cultish horror film by Harry Kümel with a cameo by Orson Welles.

ABOUT THIS BOOK

This *Explore Guide* has been produced by the editors of Insight Guides, whose books have set the standard for visual travel guides since 1970. With top-quality photography and authoritative recommendations, these guidebooks bring you the very best routes and itineraries in the world's most exciting destinations.

BEST ROUTES

The routes in the book provide something to suit all budgets, tastes and trip lengths. As well as covering the destination's many classic attractions, the itineraries track lesser-known sights, and there are also excursions for those who want to extend their visit outside the city. The routes embrace a range of interests, so whether you are an art fan, a gourmet, a history buff or have kids to entertain, you will find an option to suit.

We recommend reading the whole of a route before setting out. This should help you to familiarise yourself with it and enable you to plan where to stop for refreshments – options are shown in the 'Food and Drink' box at the end of each tour.

For our pick of the tours by theme, consult Recommended Routes for... (see pages 4–5).

INTRODUCTION

The routes are set in context by this introductory section, giving an overview of the destination to set the scene, plus background information on food and drink, shopping and more, while a succinct history timeline highlights the key events over the centuries.

DIRECTORY

Also supporting the routes is a Directory chapter, with a clearly organised A–Z of practical information, our pick of where to stay while you are there and select restaurant listings; these eateries complement the more low-key cafés and restaurants that feature within the routes and are intended to offer a wider choice for evening dining. Also included here are some nightlife listings, plus a handy language guide and our recommendations for books and films about the destination.

ABOUT THE AUTHORS

Katharine Mill lived in Belgium for a decade until 2008. Based in Brussels, she was lifestyle editor and then deputy editor of *The Bulletin*, a weekly English-language magazine, covering subjects ranging from politics and fashion to contemporary dance. Initially resistant to the charm of Bruges, she became a convert following exposure to the paintings of Jan van Eyck, a springtime walk through the Beguinage and a summer evening's cycle along the canal from Gouden Handrei to Speelmansrei. Nicholas Hirst lives in Brussels and also writes for *The Bulletin*. In 2008 he spent a year in Bruges as a researcher and now visits the city regularly for work and pleasure. Thanks also go to Jackie Staddon and Hilary Weston.

CONTACT THE EDITORS

We hope you find this Explore Guide useful, interesting and a pleasure to read. If you have any questions or feedback on the text, pictures or maps, please do let us know. If you have noticed any errors or outdated facts, or have suggestions for places to include on the routes, we would be delighted to hear from you. Please drop us an email at insight@apaguide.co.uk. Thanks!

CREDITS

Explore Bruges
Contributors: Katharine Mill, Nicholas Hirst
Commissioning Editor: Carine Tracanelli
Series Editor: Sarah Clark
Pictures/Art: Tom Smyth/Shahid Mahmood
Map Production: originial cartography
Berndston & Berndston GmbH, updated by
Apa Cartography Department
Production: Tynan Dean and Rebeka Davies

Photo credits: Alamy 22, 23, 59, 110, 111;
Apa Publications 32; Bistro Refter 94MC,
113; Bruges Tourism 5MC, 5MR, 6BC, 9,
10/11, 11R 34, 43, 45, 51, 54/55, 62,
65, 71; Corbis 2/3T, 42, 57, 106, 107,
117; De Stove 105; Dreamstime 36/37,
78, 130; Erasmus 94BC, 104, 104/105;
Fotolia 38, 52, 94BL, 95BR, 102; Georgie
Scott/Apa Publications 5MR, 24BC, 82, 83,
84, 85, 86/87, 87, 92; Getty Images 6/7T,
20/21, 24/25T, 69, 103; Glyn Genin/
Apa Publications 1, 2MR, 2BR, 2BC, 2BL,
4ML, 4BC, 6ML, 6MC, 6BL, 6MR, 6BR, 14,
14/15, 15, 16, 16/17, 18, 18/19, 19, 20,
21, 24ML, 24MC, 24BL, 26, 26/27, 27, 28,
28/29, 29, 31, 35, 36, 37, 39, 40, 40/41,
41, 44, 44/45, 46, 47, 48, 49, 52/53, 53,
56, 56/57, 58, 60, 61, 67, 68, 73, 74, 76,
78/79, 80, 92/93, 94MR, 94/95T, 97,
106/107, 108, 109, 111, 114, 115, 116,
118, 122, 123, 124, 125, 126, 126/127,
128, 129, 131, 132, 133; Gregory Wrona/
Apa Publications 4MC, 4TL, 17, 72, 88, 89,
90, 91; iStockphoto 2ML, 5TL, 8, 10, 13,
24MR, 30, 33, 50, 50/51, 54, 55, 63, 77L,
81, 84/85, 86, 93, 134, 135; Jan Darthet
121; Jerry Dennis/Apa Publications 2MC,
12, 24BR, 60/61, 64, 66, 70, 75, 76/77;
Kobal 137; Leonardo 96, 98, 99, 100,
101; Mary Evans Picture Library 136; Rex
Features 79; TIPS 119, 120; Zeno 94ML,
112, 112/113.
Cover credits: (Main) Flemish gables *Getty
Images;* (BR) Canal, *Glyn Genin/Apa Publications;* (Back) Brugge *iStockphoto*; Windmill,
iStockphoto.

Printed by CTPS — China

DISTRIBUTION

Worldwide
APA Publications GmbH & Co. Verlag KG
(Singapore branch)
7030 Ang Mo Kio Ave 5, 08-65
Northstar @ AMK, Singapore 569880
Email: apasin@singnet.com.sg
UK and Ireland
Dorling Kindersley Ltd (a Penguin Company)
80 Strand, London, WC2R 0RL, UK
Email: sales@uk.dk.com
US
Ingram Publisher Services
One Ingram Blvd, PO Box 3006, La Vergne,
TN 37086-1986
Email: ips@ingramcontent.com
Australia and New Zealand
Woodslane
10 Apollo St, Warriewood NSW 2102,
Australia
Email: info@woodslane.com.au

INDEX

MAP LEGEND

● Start of tour

→ Tour & route direction

❶ Recommended sight

❷ Recommended restaurant/café

★ Place of interest

ℹ Tourist information

🏛 Statue/monument

✉ Main post office

🚌 Main bus station

✳ Windmill

🏰 Castle / ruin

Park

Important building

Hotel

Transport hub

Shop / market

Pedestrian area

Urban area